How to Open & Operate a Financially Successful

Fashion Design Business

With Companion CD-ROM

By Janet Engle

How to Open & Operate a Financially Successful Fashion Design Business — With Companion CD-ROM

ISBN-13: 978-1-60138-225-2   ISBN-10: 1-60138-225-1

Library of Congress Cataloging-in-Publication Data

Engle, Janet.
  How to Open & Operate a Financially Successful Fashion Design Business: With Companion CD-ROM / by Janet Engle.
    p. cm.
  Includes bibliographical references and index.
  ISBN-13: 978-1-60138-225-2 (alk. paper)
  ISBN-10: 1-60138-225-1 (alk. paper)
  1. Clothing trade. 2. Fashion designers. I. Title.

  HD9940.A2E54 2008
  746.9'2068--dc22
              2008008531

INTERIOR LAYOUT DESIGN: Vickie Taylor • vtaylor@atlantic-pub.com

Printed in the United States

Printed on Recycled Paper

We recently lost our beloved pet "Bear," who was not only
our best and dearest friend but also the "Vice President of
Sunshine" here at Atlantic Publishing. He did not receive
a salary but worked tirelessly 24 hours a day to please
his parents. Bear was a rescue dog that turned around
and showered myself, my wife Sherri, his grandparents
Jean, Bob and Nancy and every person and animal he met
(maybe not rabbits) with friendship and love. He made a
lot of people smile every day.

We wanted you to know that a portion of the profits of this
book will be donated to The Humane Society of
the United States.

–*Douglas & Sherri Brown*

THE HUMANE SOCIETY
OF THE UNITED STATES ©

The human-animal bond is as old as human history. We cherish our animal companions for their unconditional affection and acceptance. We feel a thrill when we glimpse wild creatures in their natural habitat or in our own backyard.

Unfortunately, the human-animal bond has at times been weakened. Humans have exploited some animal species to the point of extinction.

The Humane Society of the United States makes a difference in the lives of animals here at home and worldwide. The HSUS is dedicated to creating a world where our relationship with animals is guided by compassion. We seek a truly humane society in which animals are respected for their intrinsic value, and where the human-animal bond is strong.

Want to help animals? We have plenty of suggestions. Adopt a pet from a local shelter, join The Humane Society and be a part of our work to help companion animals and wildlife. You will be funding our educational, legislative, investigative and outreach projects in the U.S. and across the globe.

Or perhaps you'd like to make a memorial donation in honor of a pet, friend or relative? You can through our Kindred Spirits program. And if you'd like to contribute in a more structured way, our Planned Giving Office has suggestions about estate planning, annuities, and even gifts of stock that avoid capital gains taxes.

Maybe you have land that you would like to preserve as a lasting habitat for wildlife. Our Wildlife Land Trust can help you. Perhaps the land you want to share is a backyard—that's enough. Our Urban Wildlife Sanctuary Program will show you how to create a habitat for your wild neighbors.

So you see, it's easy to help animals. And The HSUS is here to help.

The Humane Society of the United States
2100 L Street NW
Washington, DC 20037
202-452-1100
www.hsus.org

Contents

Preface...7

Chapter 1: Owning a Fashion
Design Business..11

Chapter 2: Before You Open..................................25

Chapter 3: Writing a Business Plan...................41

Chapter 4: Developing a fashion Focus...........55

Chapter 5: Designing Your Line......................69

Chapter 6: Sample Garments.............................83

Chapter 7: Selling Your Designs.......................95

Chapter 8: Manufacturing...............................109

Chapter 9: Marketing.......................................123

Chapter 10: Advertising & Publicity 135

Chapter 11: Accounting & Bookkeeping 155

Chapter 12: Budgeting & Operational
Management 165

Chapter 13: Using Technology 177

Chapter 14: Keeping Your
Customers Happy 193

Chapter 15: Staff Issues 219

Chapter 16: Business Transactions 243

Bibliography 283

Author Dedication & Biography 285

Index 287

Preface

*T*hroughout human history, most people have worn clothing that was made in their own homes. In rural households, women sewed the family apparel out of fabric woven from fiber they had spun. Styles changed slowly as women developed new techniques and patterns and then shared them with their neighbors.

By the mid-1800s, French couturiers, who were once employed only by the highest aristocracy, began to attract attention from British and American socialites. The Chambre Syndicale de la Couture Parisienne, the governing body of high fashion in France, was founded in 1868. It instituted rules to help protect couturiers' exclusive designs from being copied by mass producers. These rules established fashion as a concern of only the wealthy. Styles changed with every season, and staying en vogue was an expensive endeavor.

Paris was the heart of the fashion industry. Because of long transport times, American women at the turn of the 20th century struggled to stay in style. It was not until World War I cut off French exports that American fashion developed. Domestic production, along with the increased popularity of car travel, made fashion more accessible to the middle-class American woman. Suddenly, more customers could come to cities to buy couture-inspired clothing. Department stores and private dressmakers met the increased demand by offering semi-finished dresses, which women could have hemmed and altered to fit their figures.

During the war, women in the upper classes found the current style too restrictive for the active roles they played in patriotic and humanitarian efforts. Led by Gabrielle "Coco" Chanel, the fashion industry began producing comfortable, attractive, and functional garments. The line between day and evening wear became blurred, and the formal evening gown disappeared from the most fashionable closets.

After World War I, styles returned to more feminine lines, although women refused to give up the pockets and looser fits they had become accustomed to. Artificial fibers, such as rayon, gained acceptance, especially in the budding ready-to-wear market, and blends of natural and artificial fibers appeared.

The ready-to-wear market embraced the machines of the industrial revolution. As a result, clothing production became quicker and cheaper. Even through the Great Depression, most households purchased clothing instead of making their own. The late 1930s saw a revival of sophisticated and intricate fashions. The cinema became the major source of fashion information for the average woman. Once again, there was a clear demarcation between day and evening styles.

World War II was a challenging time for the fashion industry. Again, the world was cut off from French couture. In addition, fabric shortages and the need for factory space in Britain promoted a "make do with what you have" mentality. Clothing became rationed. Out of necessity, versatile separates came into style. Because they cost fewer ration tickets than a pair of stockings, pants became popular among women.

Postwar styles blossomed like extravagant flowers. Influenced by abstract art and modern architecture, bold prints and structured cuts were seen at the couture houses. Accessories took on a more important role. The right gloves, hat, and handbag were considered as important as the perfect dress. As the wholesale industry became more organized, ready-made clothing was produced in higher quality at an even lower cost.

While the couture houses dictated fashion for the first half of the 20th century, the late 1950s styles came from the street. Young people had more independence and money of their own. They were not afraid to modify their clothing or to use their appearance as a form of rebellion against authority. Countercultures developed their own dress codes. By their choices in clothing, people defined themselves as Beatniks, Rockers, or Mods. Fads appeared in this era, making certain accessories, colors, patterns, or designers de rigueur for brief moments.

Couture became a mixture of high-tech and Indian prints. The runways saw ultratailored and free-form cuts both. Throughout the 1960s and 1970s, the increased prevalence of women with jobs outside the home created a market for business wear and styles that worked for both day and night events. In the 1980s, working women demanded more feminine choices for their professional wardrobe. The main source of inspiration for most design houses remained street styles, and television shows overtook movies as the main way women formed opinions about fashion.

In the 1990s fashion still helped identify a person's social group; however, these groups became more complex and overlapping. An office worker by day could be a goth by night and require a wardrobe for each life style. The late 1990s and early 2000s saw advances in fiber technology. Suddenly, fabric was available to wick away moisture, protect against solar radiation, repel insects, keep out the rain while allowing the skin to breathe, hold in more heat, or any combination of these.

Currently, men and women lead complex lives that demand a variety of clothing. From work to the gym to the club, people want apparel that meets their needs while expressing individuality. Successful fashion design companies understand this and combine creativity, technical expertise, and business know-how to get new styles to the consumer.

Style has always been influenced by the technology and political situations of the times. As the owner of a fashion design business, you will help shape where the industry goes next.

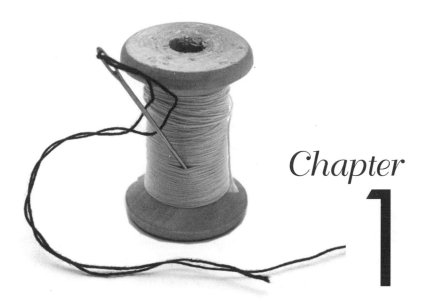

Chapter

1

Owning a Fashion Design Business

Clothing makes up a large portion of the fashion industry. People need clothes for work, play, sports, special occasions, and sleeping, but apparel is only one part of fashion design. Accessories, home fashions, and "Do It Yourself" (DIY) patterns are other segments of the industry.

Accessories are the shoes, socks, hats, scarves, belts, purses, gloves, and jewelry that complement apparel. Companies may specialize in designing one type of accessory, or they may branch out into several categories. Some apparel designers cross-merchandise clothing and accessories within a single line. This is a way of presenting a unified look. Designers hope customers will like the image and purchase both the apparel and the accessories.

Home fashion is a growing crossover market for apparel designers. People relax, entertain, and even work in their homes. Large companies such as Donna Karen and Ralph Lauren now produce bedding and furniture in addition to their clothing lines. The home fashion industry includes bed, bath, and table coverings; area rugs; window and wall treatments; and upholstered furniture.

The DIY fashion industry provides materials, instructions, and patterns for people who want to make their own apparel, accessories, or home fashions. Designers select coordinated bead kits, fabric, or fiber lines using their professional knowledge of color, texture, pattern, and current trends. Sewing patterns and fiber art kits are other segments of the DIY fashion industry.

How Fashion is Sold

The success of your business relies on how well you sell your designs. The fashion industry can be divided into two markets: wholesale and retail.

Wholesale

Wholesale businesses sell their lines to retailers, who then market the fashions to the end user. Designers can show their apparel to buyers through trade shows, market weeks, and market centers.

Trade shows are conventions sponsored by trade associations or independent trade show producers. Designers rent booth space where they can demonstrate their lines and meet with representatives from retail businesses. Attendants may also attend workshops, lectures, and panel discussions about trends and industry concerns.

Market weeks are held many times throughout the year. Most focus on only one category of fashion, for example, swimwear or children's clothing.

During market weeks, buyers for retail businesses can view fashion lines and meet with sales representatives to purchase merchandise for their stores.

Market centers are buildings that house permanent showrooms in which retail buyers can review fashion lines. Market centers may include temporary showroom space that designers can rent for short periods of time.

Retail

Any business that sells apparel to the end user is a retailer. Retailers differ in size, organization, and target market. If you plan on selling your designs directly to your customers, other fashion retailers will be your competition. If you plan on selling your designs through national chains, these retailers will be your clients. In either case, it is important to understand the most common types of places where apparel is sold.

Department stores are large retailers that sell a wide range of products, grouped in sections, or departments. They serve a wide range of customers and carry both national brands and private labels. Department stores are important to the fashion industry. Their sales account for more than $.20 of every dollar buyers spend on apparel. Examples of department stores include Sears and Kohl's.

Specialty stores, such as Talbots and Ann Taylor, are retailers that focus on just a few categories of merchandise. However, they carry a large assortment of colors, sizes, and styles within those categories. These stores have well-defined target markets. Like department stores, they may also carry national brands or private labels.

Discount retailers are like department stores in that they offer many types of products to a broad target market. However, discount retailers price merchandise at budget prices. Discount retailers such as Kmart, Target, and Wal-Mart have their own labels of apparel, but they also carry some national brands.

Off-price retailers sell national brands at discount prices. Off-price retailers include:

- Factory outlet stores, where manufacturers sell seconds and overruns directly to customers

- Independent off-price retailers, which sell national brand seconds and overruns

- Retailer-owned outlet stores, where department and specialty stores sell returned and clearance merchandise

- Closeout stores, which sell merchandise from liquidations

- Sample stores, which sell sample merchandise that is no longer needed

Not all fashion sales occur in a traditional store. Alternative retailers account for more than 6 percent of clothing sales. These types of transactions include mail order and catalog, Internet, television-based, and at-home or "party plan" sales.

Alternative retailers have many advantages over traditional business models. Customers can purchase through a Web site on their own schedules. They do not have to wait for a store to open and hope that what they are looking for is in stock. Alternative retail models may be less expensive to own and operate than traditional stores, which can allow the online and catalog businesses to offer merchandise at a lower price than a store that has to pay rent to the mall.

Because of these advantages, department stores, specialty stores, and discount retailers may complement their store sales with alternative strategies. However, alternative retailers are at a disadvantage to their traditional counterparts in many ways. Customers may not want to wait for merchandise to be delivered. Instead, they may prefer to drive to a store and have their clothing immediately. In addition, customers cannot touch and try on clothing in a catalog or on a Web site. They may not want to deal with the hassle of returning the merchandise if it does not fit.

At-home or "party plan" retailers show samples of their fashions in the homes of potential customers. Customers can place orders based on what they see. At-home retail experiences can include trunk shows, where designers demonstrate their entire lines. Trunk shows can also be special events at retail establishments.

Which is Best for You?

As the owner of a fashion design business, you will have to decide how you will get your clothes to the consumers. Will you market your lines to stores or set up a retail shop yourself? If you decide to retail your own clothes, will you sell them online, open a traditional storefront, or rely on home sales?

The best strategy for you depends on several factors. Unless you are willing to travel, it may be hard to show your clothes to national retailers if you do not live near a market center or a city that hosts trade shows. If you have limited startup capital, you may not be able to fulfill large orders from a department store chain.

Some fashion designers want to keep the security and income of their day jobs but pursue fashion on a part-time basis. Selling designs through local trunk shows or on consignment through local boutiques are ways to operate your business part time. If you want complete freedom to market your apparel to customers, you may decide to open your own clothing store.

Professional Outlook

In many ways, there has never been a better time to open a fashion design business. Many people want clothing that tells something about their interests and life styles and are willing to pay a premium for high-quality clothes that are different than what their friends are wearing. The Internet makes it easy for customers to find specialty designers and place orders. Consumers do not have to settle for the limited selection at their local department store.

Designer clothing is a luxury item. When money is short, consumers might cut their apparel budget. Because of this, the fashion industry is dependent on the health of local, national, and even international economies.

Professional Organizations

The following organizations provide information and learning opportunities for fashion designers and fashion design business owners:

- The International Association of Clothing Designers and Executives (**www.iacde.com**)

- The Fashion Group International (**www.fgi.org**)

- The Council of Fashion Designers of America (**www.cfda.com**)

- The Costume Designers Guild (**www.costumedesignersguild.com**)

- The American Apparel and Footwear Association (**www.apparelandfootwear.org**)

- The International Apparel Federation (**www.iafnet.com**)

Joining a professional organization can be a good way to become involved in the industry and network with suppliers, manufacturers, and other designers.

What to Expect as a Fashion Design Business Owner

Operating a fashion design business can be a remarkable creative experience. An entire line can be developed from a single moment of inspiration, and, as the owner, you direct the process. Your visions could end up on runways or in stores on the other side of the world.

The fashion industry goes beyond artistry and glamour. You may hire experts and consult with specialists, but you are the final decision-maker. If a designer you hire selects the wrong fabric, you might lose a season's worth of sales. If your accountant gives you poor financial advice, you might pay substantial tax penalties. In either situation, as the boss, you are ultimately responsible and will have to deal with the consequences.

Benefits of Owning a Fashion Design Business

As a business owner, you decide how to focus your energy and resources every day. You can organize your schedule around other responsibilities. Unless you are meeting with a customer, consultant, or supplier, much of your work can be done at any time. If you design the perfect custom wedding dress, your client will not care if you sketch in your office during traditional business hours or in your pajamas at midnight.

In addition to this flexibility, owning a fashion design business gives you an opportunity to turn your passion into your livelihood. Equipment and materials that are too costly for a hobbyist's budget are business expenses and potential tax write-offs to your company.

Disadvantages of Owning a Fashion Design Business

Starting and running a business can take more time than you expect. Between organizing marketing campaigns, following up with customers, negotiating contracts, paying bills, tracking down shipments, reviewing the latest labeling regulations, and balancing your ledger, you might not have enough time left to design fashions.

A business can be expensive. You might not make a profit for several years. Even if your business is profitable, you will not be able to count on a certain income every month. Unless you have a day job with benefits, you will have to organize your own health insurance and retirement savings plan.

The "Average" Day of a Business Owner

As a business owner, you may play many different roles in your company. One day you may be the human resources manager, interviewing prospective designers. The next day you might be the bookkeeper, updating the financial records. You may have to dress professionally while you meet with a potential investor, then change into edgier attire to project the right image to a client. You need to be equally comfortable talking on the telephone as you are in front of the sketchbook.

Some days, you might find yourself on an emotional roller coaster. After weeks of research, you might finally stumble on the perfect fabric for a design, only to find that the mill has just discontinued it. The thrill of landing a large contract with a major retail chain might be tempered by the realization that now you have to fulfill that order.

Skills for Success

If you are artistic and interested in fashion, working for yourself may sound tailor made for you. Owning a design business requires more than creativity. Business and technical skills are important cornerstones needed to build a financially successful business.

Communication

Communication skills are important to any business owner. As a designer, you will need to talk with your current and potential clients. You will have to understand what they want, what they like about a piece, and what should be changed even if they do not tell you explicitly. Fashion designers have to talk with the retail buyers who place their work in department stores and boutiques, suppliers who sell cloth and accessories, and contractors who will take that fabric and sew the designed apparel.

As a business owner, you will need to be able to relate to other professionals, such as bankers, lawyers, and accountants. You need to be able to tell them your requirements and to understand their advice.

Leadership

The owner of a fashion design business has a much different role than a designer who works for an employer. As a business owner, it is your job to guide your company. Even if you surround yourself with a professional and highly qualified staff, you will need to take charge and make the decisions that direct the growth of your business.

Effective leaders do not dictate every single detail. Micromanaging projects can lower staff morale and cost your business valuable team members. Good leadership is a balance between giving your employees independence and realizing that the future of the business is your responsibility.

Perseverance

Creating a line of clothing can be a time consuming job. For many companies, the process of conceiving a design, putting it onto paper, creating a pattern, choosing fabric, sewing a prototype, making any necessary changes, and constructing the final garment can take up to two years. Unless you already have a name in the fashion industry, it may take you a while to find your niche and build clientele.

Organization

When you start a fashion design business, you will generate paperwork. Unless you have a way to organize your files, you might misplace important financial data, legal information, employee records, order forms, receipts, designs, marketing ideas, or contracts. As your business grows, you will need to juggle several projects at the same time. Organization will be crucial.

Technical Skills

There are several technical skills you will need as the owner of a fashion design business. You should be able to sketch out your ideas. There is no better way to communicate your designs to clients or staff members.

Even if you do not plan on personally making the clothing you design, you should know enough about sewing and patternmaking to work with your construction staff. You will need to be able to tell them exactly what needs to be done to achieve your desired look.

Creativity

Fashion is a crowded field. There are many designers competing for retail and wholesale customers. Landing big contracts can be hard for new companies because some buyers prefer to work with established firms with proven track records.

If you have a unique voice within the industry, then you have a better chance of standing out and attracting clients. Successful designers do not just respond to trends — they help shape the path of fashion. Creativity is not only important in your designs, but also the more innovative you are in marketing your business and solving operational problems, the better your chances of being successful.

Putting the Skills Together

Operating a successful fashion design business requires a varied set of skills. You need to be creative enough to produce designs that appeal to your customers while staying within your operational budget. You will need to research your target market, interpret the data to create designs that will appeal to your potential customers, communicate with patternmakers and manufacturers to get the apparel made, negotiate contracts with suppliers and buyers, and keep your records, appointments, and deadlines organized.

If you do not have confidence in your technical, creative, or business skills, consider pairing with a partner who brings to the table the abilities you lack. If you are determined to build your fashion design business by yourself, you may want to take some time to increase your knowledge about fashion or garment construction. There are many ways to learn the technical and artistic skills needed to operate a fashion design business.

There are more than 200 colleges and private art schools with programs accredited by the National Association of Schools of Art and Design (NASAD). Whether you pursue a degree or just take a few courses, fashion design classes can help you learn how to sketch, improve your design aesthetic, and increase your familiarity with textiles. Some programs offer business classes that focus on the fashion industry. To find out if a program is accredited, visit **http://nasad.arts-accredit.org**.

If you are confident in your technical skills, consider an accounting, management, entrepreneurship, or marketing course. Even after you start your fashion design business, continuing education can give you more tricks in your designer toolbox, provide the opportunity to network in the local fashion community, and give you more ways to approach business issues.

Education does not have to mean going back to school. Some of the most practical skills are those that can be learned hands on. Working for another designer, for example, will give you a firsthand look at how the fashion world operates. Whether you are a patternmaker, sewer, researcher, salesperson, or "gofer," you will be able to see which leadership and communication tactics work and which you will avoid once you are in charge. If you cannot find a job with a designer, consider an unpaid internship or apprenticeship. The experience you gain could be valuable.

Perhaps the easiest way to learn about fashion design is to start designing for yourself, your family, and your friends. This is how Elsa Schiaparelli, one of the most influential designers of casual wear in the 20th century, got her start. Even if you are working for a relative and receiving payment only for the cost of the fabric, treat every design opportunity like a professional project. Take the time to talk with your clients so you can define their needs and wants. Try to translate these desires into your design. Present your designs to your clients and encourage their honest feedback. Practice patternmaking and sewing, and be sure to take plenty of notes. Every project, no matter how small it seems, can be a chance to learn and grow as a designer. Keep a portfolio of your successes to show to future clients.

CASE STUDY: DAVE BROWN HATS

Dave Brown, Owner
Dave Brown Hats
www.davebrownhats.com
3054 West Henrietta Road
Rochester, NY 14623
info@davebrownhats.com

My family has been in dry cleaning for 75 years. My father was always working with hats — drying, cleaning, blocking, and shaping them. I bought some hat-making equipment from a business that went out of business, but I did not know what I was doing.

I saw Steve Martin, no relation to the actor, when I was at a hat store in New York City. I asked to watch him work, and he thought it was nice that someone wanted to learn. I ended up apprenticing with him. He was a hard taskmaster. I would take in pieces that I thought were pretty nice, and he would tear them apart.

After about five years, Steve looked at a hat I made, tossed it on a table, and said, "You're a hatter."

Now, my hats have been used in more than 20 movies. I have always tried to be nice to costumers and assistants. Whether a hat is going to be for a movie, a celebrity, or an ordinary person, my name is going on that hat, and I make it with the same quality.

CASE STUDY: DAVE BROWN HATS

Everyone wants to be Hank Williams, but no one wants to die. You have to pay your dues to put out good products. You have to crawl before you walk and walk before you run.

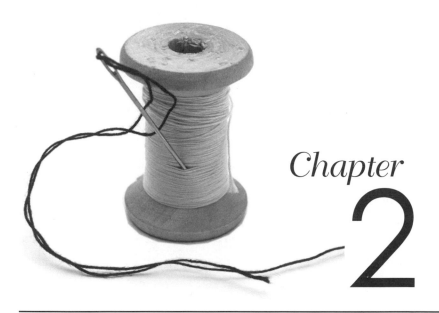

Chapter

2

Before You Open

Once you have decided you have the skills and vision needed to make your design business a success, you might feel tempted to break out your sketchbook, go shopping for fabric, and call up some friends to model for your first fashion show.

The right time to make business decisions and organize the legalities of your company is before you open for business. A little preparation and planning at this stage may save you money, time, and problems in the future.

Organizing Your Business

As a business owner, one of the first decisions you need to make is your legal relationship with the business. There are three types of businesses: sole proprietorships, partnerships, and corporations.

Sole Proprietorships

If you do not file any paperwork to notify the government otherwise, your business is a sole proprietorship. This means that any profits from the business are your personal income and are subject to income tax. In addition, you are liable for all business debts, even if they exceed your investment in the company. If your business cannot pay its bills, you will have to use your personal income or property.

In a sole proprietorship, one person owns the business and any associated property. This form of business is easier to form and to dissolve than a partnership and a corporation.

Partnerships

You may need the experience, skills, or money of another person or group to get your business started. A partnership offers the convenience of a sole proprietorship with the ability to share the ownership and liability of the business between two or more people.

If you form a partnership, you should write up an agreement, or articles of partnership, to be agreed on and signed by all the partners. This agreement should include:

- How much money each partner will contribute to the business

- How any profit or loss will be divided between the partners

- The extent of decision-making abilities each partner will have

- The responsibilities of each partner in the day-to-day operations of the business

🖈 Dissolution procedures in case a partner dies or wants to leave the business

Like sole proprietorships, partnerships are easy to form. Also like sole proprietorships, the parties involved in a partnership are responsible for any debts incurred by the business.

Disagreements may arise when two or more partners must come to a consensus about important business decisions. However, having different ideas and skill sets can lead to a highly creative and effective atmosphere.

Corporations

Unlike a sole proprietorship or partnership, a corporation is considered separate from its owners for legal purposes. Corporations are owned by stockholders, and each owner's liability for any of the debts is limited to that owner's initial investment.

Corporation stockholders elect a board of directors to govern the business. The day-to-day operations are handled by the corporate officers, who are appointed by the board of directors. Stockholders receive their share of the profits in the form of dividends.

There are two types of corporation structures geared toward small businesses. Subchapter S corporations have fewer than 75 shareholders. In a traditional corporation, or C corporation, income is taxed both as personal income to the shareholder and as profit for the company. Income from subchapter S corporations, however, is taxed only as personal income. In addition, losses from the business can be used to offset other personal income. This can add up to significant tax savings, especially when a business is just getting started.

Another type of corporate structure to consider is a limited liability corporation (LLC). The LLC structure has the limited liability benefits of a corporation, but profit or loss is considered personal income.

Which is Best for You?

You should consider whether you prefer the freedom to open, operate, and close your business that a sole proprietorship offers or the security of limited personal liability that comes from owning a corporation. In addition, consult a lawyer or tax advisor to review your current economic position and the future goals for the company. There may be a significant financial benefit to a particular business structure.

Choosing a Name

Another important decision you have to make early in your planning is the name for your fashion design business. What you call your business may influence many other future decisions, such as your logo, marketing image, and Web site address.

Start by making a list of possibilities. You can include some variations of your own name or lists of your favorite colors, animals, places, and even foods. Use this list to develop different combinations. You will be seeing your business name daily. It will appear on your stationary, receipts, mailing labels, hangtags, contracts, packages, and signs, so cross off any choices you do not like.

Now search the Internet or use a trademark search service to find out which choices are already being used by other companies. The United States Patent and Trademark Office has an online database of pending and granted trademarks that you can access through its Web site at **www.uspto. gov**. You want your business name to identify you, not to confuse potential customers or send them to a competitor.

Think about the type of customer you hope will buy your designs. Would any of the choices left on your list offend them? Cross those names off. Are any particularly appealing or memorable? Consumers tend to remember names that are descriptive, humorous, or unexpected.

Think about the image you want for your business. Do you want potential customers to see you as artsy, earthy, sophisticated, fresh, or sexy? The name you choose should reflect that image.

Once you choose a business name, your state or local laws may require that you receive a "doing business as," or DBA, license. The DBA may be part of the standard business license application, or it may be separate.

You may also want to register your business name as a trademark with the United States Patent and Trademark Office through the Trademark Electronic Application System at **www.uspto.gov**.

Laws, Regulations, and Licenses

Business regulations differ by state and city. Check with your local department of business development or taxation to determine what licenses and permits you may need.

In many states, you need to apply for a resale license or sales tax license. This is usually required if you are selling tangible goods. When you buy tax-exempt, wholesale supplies, you need to have this number. In addition, you need this number to file sales tax on any goods you sell.

You may also need a city or county business license. If you have any employees, you need an IRS employer identification number (EIN). You can apply for an EIN online at **IRS.gov** or use Form SS-4, "Application for Employer Identification Number," which is included on the accompanying CD.

If you live in California or New York and are manufacturing the designs you sell, you may need a garment manufacturing license. You can apply for this certificate through your state department of labor.

Insurance

As a business owner, you may be responsible for any injuries incurred by your employees or customers on your premises. Without adequate insurance coverage, this puts your business and possibly your personal belongings at risk.

If you are running your fashion design business from your home, contact your homeowner's or renter's insurance provider to see if your current policy will cover your business operations.

You may want, or be legally required, to carry extra insurance on your expensive equipment, liability insurance in case of accidents, worker's compensation and health insurance for yourself or your employees, or disability insurance in case an injury or illness prevents you from running your business.

Equipment, Furnishings, and Supplies

The equipment you need to start a fashion design business depends on what you are producing and how much work you intend to contract out.

Office equipment includes:

- Computer

- Stationery (letterhead, business cards, printer paper)

- Computer desk and chair

- Fax machine

- Scanner

- Printer

- Copy machine

- File cabinet

- Telephone

- Planner or wall calendar

- Accounting and payroll software

Basic design studios may need:

- Sketch books in several sizes

- Drawing pencils and erasers

- Watercolors, colored pencils, or felt-tip pens

- Loose, high-quality drawing paper for final drawings

- Light table for tracing

- Foam boards and adhesives for storyboards

- Rulers, compasses, protractors, and other drafting supplies

- Design or graphics software

❧ Fabric/fiber

If you will be manufacturing the clothes you sell, you may need:

❧ Sewing machine

❧ Serger

❧ Knitting machine

❧ Linker

❧ Shelving and storage

❧ Cutting table

❧ Workbench

❧ Directional lighting

❧ Notions

❧ Embroidery machine

❧ Dressmaking or tailor's bust form

❧ Pattern paper

❧ Grader's set square

❧ Fabric/fiber

If you plan to consult with clients, you may need additional furniture and decorations to keep your workspace comfortable and professional:

- Comfortable seating for client and guest

- Directional lighting

- Easel to display storyboard

- Table

- Rug or carpeting

- Wall decorations

- Window treatments

Financing Your Business

You can spend years perfecting your skills and polishing your business plan, but when you begin operating your fashion design business, you will need money. How much startup capital you require depends on the focus of your business, how large you intend to start, the image you want to cultivate, and your creativity.

How Much Money Will You Need?

To find out how much startup money you should pursue, you need to calculate how much you need to get your business running. Use the following worksheet, also found on the accompanying CD, to add up the potential expenses.

ESTIMATED STARTUP COSTS

Licensing, Registration, and Legal Fees

- Resale license
- Garment manufacturing license
- Trademark registration
- Insurance

- Business license
- "Doing business as" certificate
- Incorporation fees
- Other fees

Office Equipment & Supplies

- Computer
- Desk and chair
- Scanner
- Copy machine
- Telephone
- Accounting/payroll software

- Stationery
- Fax machine
- Printer
- File cabinet
- Planner or wall calendar
- Other office needs

Design Supplies

- Art supplies
- File cabinet
- Design software
- Other design needs

- Light table
- Drafting supplies
- Fabric/fiber

Manufacturing Equipment & Supplies

- Sewing machine
- Knitting machine
- Shelving & storage
- Workbench
- Notions
- Dressmaker's form
- Fabric/fiber
- Other manufacturing needs

- Serger
- Linker
- Cutting table
- Directional lighting
- Embroidery machine
- Pattern paper
- Grader's set square

ESTIMATED STARTUP COSTS

Consultation Equipment & Supplies

- Seating
- Display easel
- Decorations
- Other consultation needs
- Lighting
- Floor coverings
- Window treatments

Initial Marketing Expenses

- Print advertisements
- Online advertisements
- Other marketing expenses
- Web site construction
- Printing

Building & Utilities Costs

- Rent deposit
- Utility deposits
- 3 months' utilities
- Renovations
- 3 months' rent
- Other building & utilities costs

TOTAL ESTIMATED STARTUP COSTS

Where Can You Cut Costs?

Adding up your estimated startup costs can be an eye-opening experience. You may realize that the fashion design business of your dreams is well within your financial reach, or you may be daunted by the projected costs.

If the estimated expenses are higher than you expected, you may be able to cut costs without sacrificing the quality of your business.

Consider buying used office and manufacturing equipment and supplies instead of new. Look for bargains at auctions and liquidation sales. Dealers can be a good source for pre-owned equipment, as some people trade in smaller or less complicated machines when they can afford better. Dealers may offer a service plan or warranty on used goods.

If you plan to start small, you may be able to get by with "hobbyist equipment" — machines manufactured and marketed toward the home sewer. Hobbyist equipment may not be as durable or versatile as professional or industrial machines, but it is significantly less expensive and may be suitable until you can afford to upgrade.

You may also be able to rent expensive equipment or share the cost with another designer. If this is not possible, consider contracting out work instead of buying highly specialized machines.

You may find it more economical and space-efficient to purchase multifunction machines. An all-in-one copier, printer, scanner, and fax machine, for example, may be cheaper than buying each component separately.

Take the time to get several quotes for any equipment or service. With patience and research, you might find significant savings.

Types of Financing

The perceived or real lack of money is the main reason most business dreams never become reality. If you honestly believe in your talent and skills and are committed to making your business a financial success, you can find a way to secure the needed funds.

Personal Savings

When you start your business using personal funds, you have complete control over how the money is used. Repaying a loan can cause cash flow issues in a new business, so using your own money can reduce the amount you pay in monthly bills.

Tapping into your personal savings also has a downside. There is no guarantee that your fashion design business will make money at first or at all. Although knowing that your hard-earned cash is on the line can keep you motivated, it can also be stressful.

Although personal savings is the first place to look for startup capital, you do not have to be wealthy to start a fashion design business.

Income From a Job

If you do not have adequate startup capital saved up to start your business, consider supplementing your business with money from your current job or getting a second job to fund your operations.

If you decide to finance your business using income from a job, be sure the earmarked funds go directly to your business checking account so they are not accidentally used for personal expenses.

Private Loans

Private loans include money from family or friends that is given with the expectation of repayment. Private loans may come with lower interest rates, laxer qualification requirements, and more flexible repayment schemes than bank loans, but they may come with a significant overhead in other forms. Even if you are diligent in paying back the money, the lenders may assume that their investment entitles them to input in your business decisions. If you miss a payment, you may hurt the relationship.

If you decide to accept a private loan, make sure that both you and the lender agree to the terms, including the duration of the loan, interest rate, amount of monthly payment, and rights of the lender.

Loans Against Personal Property

You may be able to tap into equity in your home or business property to help finance your business. If you close your business for any reason, you will still need to pay this money back or risk foreclosure. In addition, if the property values in your area go down, you might find yourself owing more on the property than it is worth.

Retirement Funds

If you have a retirement fund such as a 401(k) or an IRA, you may be able to borrow money from your savings. Although individual plans vary, you can usually borrow up to half of your balance with a cap at $50,000. After you apply, the money usually comes to you quickly and without any credit check.

There are some significant disadvantages to borrowing from your retirement fund. Any money you take out of your account stops accumulating, and you may be unable to add to your savings plan until you pay the loan back. If you do not pay the loan back within the specified time, you may be hit with staggering penalties and taxes.

Personal Credit Cards

Personal credit cards are a fast and easy way to infuse funds into your business. Credit cards are available to people with a large range of credit ratings and can be used to purchase equipment, pay bills, or even access cash. Low monthly payments can be attractive to new businesses experiencing cash flow problems.

All this convenience comes with a high price tag. Credit cards usually have a higher interest rate than bank or personal loans. If you are late with or miss a payment, your interest rate may grow even higher. A high balance on a credit card can be hard and expensive to pay off, especially if you are paying the minimum monthly payment.

Bank Loans

Obtaining startup money from a bank or other lending institution can be difficult for first-time business owners. Banks prefer to lend to people with a proven track record of making money and paying back their debts. With a well-researched business plan, good personal credit history, and appropriate collateral, securing a bank loan is not impossible.

If you have a relationship with a particular bank, that is a good starting place. Most loans are negotiable, so do not be afraid to ask for specific repayment terms. If a bank turns you down, ask for feedback about how you can improve your application. Give any suggestions or criticisms serious consideration before you apply again at the same or a different bank.

The Small Business Association (SBA) can help business owners secure bank loans by guaranteeing the repayment. For more information about receiving a guaranteed loan, contact the SBA:

Small Business Association
www.sba.gov
800-827-5722

Nonprofit Organizations

Some nonprofit organizations provide funds to business owners that meet specific qualifications based on ethnicity, geographic location, gender, or income. These funds may be in the form of grants or low-interest loans.

In addition to financing, some organizations provide mentoring programs, workshops, or educational material to help business owners succeed.

The SBA has a microloan program available to new or growing businesses. Through the program, business owners apply directly to community-based nonprofit lenders for loans of less than $35,000. The lenders usually require collateral and a personal guarantee from the business owner. The SBA helps finance the loans and, in return, requires the lending institution to provide training and help to the business owners. Some lenders require you to complete training before you can receive the funding. The maximum term of these microloans is six years. Interest rates vary.

Business development organizations often find themselves with more worthy applicants than they can afford to finance. If you decide to apply for a loan from a nonprofit organization, do your research. Make sure your business meets the criteria to receive the funds. If letters of recommendation are required, choose your references carefully. Avoid family and friends and instead use people who are unbiased judges of your business potential. Employers, teachers, and coworkers are good choices. If the organization wants to know how you will spend the money, create a detailed report based on multiple estimates. If the money will be used for a major purchase, renovation, or project, include projections about how your business will benefit.

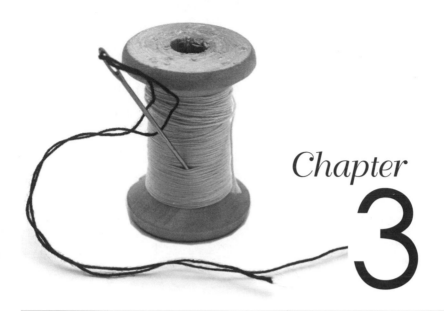

Chapter

3

Writing a Business Plan

A business plan is a formal, written document that explains how a business will run. It covers the financial, operational, and marketing details and future goals. A business plan can take many forms, depending on the organization and needs of the business.

Creating a business plan can help you organize your ideas, see how they fit together, and determine feasible goals for the near future and for the long run. Once you have a working business plan, it can serve as a map to keep your business on track. If you plan on applying for a loan, potential investors will want to see your business plan. Not having one is a sign that you do not take your business seriously.

Do You Need a Business Plan?

Even if you do not need external financing, a business plan can be a useful internal tool. The following are ways companies of all sizes can use their business plans:

- To make sure all in the organization know their roles

- To research potential competitors and determine a way to differentiate from them

- To define marketing goals

- To predict short- and long-term cash flow

- To compare financial predictions to actual performance

- To see holes in financial, marketing, and operational planning

- To focus the purpose of the business, including what products will be sold to whom

- To calculate how much money you will need to keep the business operational

- To set performance goals to make the business profitable

When Should You Write a Business Plan?

Optimally, you should have your business plan completed before you sketch your first design or buy your first bolt of cloth. Your business plan will help you see how much money you will have to proceed with your operations. The marketing section will help gel the image of your business, which will be key in the creation of a cohesive line. If you are working with one or more partners, your plan will help reduce friction by making sure all involved know their assigned roles.

Unfortunately, new business owners tend to wait until their business has grown too big to manage before they write a plan. They construct a business plan to address problems, not to prevent them.

It is never too late to write a business plan, but it is also never too early to get started. Your business plan is a tool. Do not be afraid to revise it to meet your business needs. A good business plan should grow and change with your business.

What You Will Need to Get Started

In order to write a complete business plan, you will need the following documents:

- Résumés for all the owners, corporate officers, and key personnel. Include their work histories, educational background, professional affiliations, honors related to fashion, and any special skills.

- Financial statements for the owners and corporate officers. Include lists of assets, liabilities, and income and expenditure statements.

- Personal and business credit reports for the owners and corporate officers

- Copies of equipment or property leases

- Letters of reference from business associates or other people who can assess your professional skills. Avoid using family members.

- Copies of current business contracts, such as purchase orders or loans

- A copy of your business license

- A copy of your insurance policy

- The business's articles of incorporation or partnership agreement

- Trademarks

- Licensing agreements

- Any research you have gathered about your target market

A checklist of the items you will need is on the accompanying CD.

Business Writing Guidelines

When writing your business plan, consider the potential audience. Your business plan should not be geared toward your clients, your design professor, or potential retail outlets. The financiers, business people, and potential investors who will read your business plan may care more about your financial potential than your design skills.

Make sure that the numbers you use in your financial projections are accurate and that your estimates are reasonable. Avoid exaggerations, both in your calculations and in how you describe your business. Financiers will not be convinced your business is a good credit risk just because you are sure everyone will want one of your skirts. Use your market research and competitive analysis to convince them that your product will stand out and that your business will make money.

Do not use more words in your business plan than you have to. You may hope that a lending officer will be impressed by a thick binder stuffed with papers, but this strategy will backfire once they realize you are padding your plan. They may suspect you are trying to hide something about the business.

Organize your business plan so information is easy to locate. A potential investor who has to search through five sections to learn what your business does is more likely to become frustrated than to sign a loan agreement.

Be sure to proofread your business plan before you have it bound. After you have proofed a draft, put it away for a few days, and then read through it again. Be sure to review the entire plan, including résumés and financial calculations. A spelling mistake here or there may not be a deal breaker, but a misplaced decimal point in the wrong cell of a spreadsheet can make a thriving company look as if it is struggling.

Parts of a Business Plan

A way to make the important information in your business plan easy to locate is to use the following standard organization:

1. Cover sheet

2. Executive summary

3. Statement of purpose

4. Description of business

5. Industry overview

6. Competition analysis

7. Marketing strategy

8. Operating procedures

9. Personnel

10. Financial data

Cover Sheet

Your cover sheet should give your business name, logo, and contact information. If you have bound hard copies, number each copy so you can keep track of where it is. Your cover sheet should be easy to read and attractive, but do not go overboard in an attempt to stand out. Your designs should show your creativity, and your business plan should highlight your professional side.

Executive Summary

The executive summary hits the main topics from the entire plan:

- What is the business?

- What is the purpose of the business plan?

- Who is running the business?

- Where will the business be located?

- Why is there a need for the business?

- How will the business make money or pay back the loan?

Although it is the first page in the body of the business plan, it should be the last part written.

Statement of Purpose

Why are you writing a business plan? Will you be using it internally or externally? Is it to support your loan application or to guide your long-term marketing plans?

Description of the Business

This section details the facts about your business:

- What is the name of the business?

- How long has the business operated?

- What products are you going to sell?

- From where will the business operate?

- How did the business get started?

- What is the legal form of the business?

- What is the current situation of the business?

- Who founded the business? What experience or expertise do they have in the industry? Do the founders remain involved in the business operation?

- What are the future goals of the business?

Industry Overview

This section should answer basic questions about the fashion industry and your niche in it. For example:

- How much money does the industry generate?

- What is the outlook for the industry?

- How large is your target market of potential customers?

- How much does that market contribute to the industry performance?

- Is your market expected to recede or grow?

You can research these questions by contacting trade organizations, reading business research publications, and performing surveys and interviews within your target market.

Some sources for information within the fashion industry include:

- U.S. Department of Labor, Bureau of Labor Statistics (**www.bls.gov**)

- The American Apparel and Footwear Association (**www. apparelandfootwear.org**)

- U.S. Census Bureau, County Business Patterns (**www.census.gov/ prod/www/abs/cbptotal.html**)

- U.S. Census Bureau, Economic Census (**www.census.gov/econ/ census02**)

- U.S. Census Bureau, Monthly Retail Trade and Food Services (**www. census.gov/mrts/www/mrts.html**)

- U.S. Census Bureau, Current Industrial Reports (CIR) MQ313A-Textiles (**www.census.gov/cir/www/313/mq313a.html**)

- The International Trade Administration, Office of Textiles and Apparel (**http://otexa.ita.doc.gov/msrpoint.htm**)

In addition, you may find information at your local library, small business development center, fashion design school, or chamber of commerce.

Competition Analysis

To make your business a success, you should know what your competition is doing and how well it is working. When writing this section of your business plan, your competition includes:

- Other businesses selling similar designs

- Other companies marketing to retail or wholesale establishments where you hope to place your line

- Other fashion design businesses whose products are marketed to your intended end users

Focus on what will separate your business from the competition:

- How will your designs differ from what is already on the market?

- Why will retail buyers prefer your products?

- What potential end users are being neglected by the competition?

Marketing Strategy

How you plan on marketing your line is closely tied to how you distinguish yourself from the competition. Some ways you might be different from your competition include:

- **Location**. If retailers are importing similar styles, you might be able to convince them of the value of purchasing your clothes instead.

- **Materials**. Your styles may be made out of higher-quality, less-expensive, or environmentally friendly fibers.

- **Pricing**. You might price your garments to appeal to a different population than your competitors.

- **Style**. Your designs are significantly different than what is currently on the market.

One way to think of marketing is that it is the process of educating your potential customers about how your products are better than what is available. Specific marketing techniques are detailed later in the book. The marketing section of your business plan should answer the following questions:

- How much are you going to invest in marketing?

- How will your marketing budget be divided between advertisements, public relations, and special events?

- Where will you advertise? How often? How will those publications help you reach your target market?

- What specific goals do you hope to meet through your marketing?

- Why is your strategy the most efficient use of your marketing budget?

↟ How will your marketing plan change in the next five years?

Operating Procedures

In this section, you will address the functions and expenses of the business. This includes a description of the location of the business and the initial expenditures associated with running the business. Initial expenditures might include:

↟ Business licenses and local permits

↟ Utility deposits

↟ Property renovations

↟ Furniture, equipment, and signs

↟ Business supplies

Ongoing procedures are also included in this section:

↟ How often will payroll be run?

↟ What method of bookkeeping will be used?

↟ How will transactions be processed?

↟ How much inventory will be kept?

↟ What types of inventory tracking processes will be used?

↟ What criteria will be used to hire employees?

Personnel

Include a short biography for each of the key people involved in the business. Focus on the experiences, education, skills, and certifications that make them qualified. Include each person's title, describe what parts of the operations each person will be responsible for, and list salaries.

If you plan on having any employees, list the job description for each position. Include details such as the pay rate, any training provided, and key duties.

Financial Data

If the business is already operational, describe the current financial situation with details such as:

- Average number of sales per month

- Breakdown of sales by category

- Average amount of transaction, by category

List any assumptions used to calculate your projected financial data. Summarize your estimated gross revenue and net income after taxes for the next five years.

List the capital expenditures needed to get your business off the ground and tell where the money will come from. If you are using this business plan to support a loan application, describe in detail how the loan money will be used, why the business needs the money, what other money will be used to finance the operation, and how the loan will be paid back.

The financial data should be used to calculate the following accounting documents:

- **Balance sheets**. Comparisons of the assets and liabilities, including equity, depreciation, and accounts receivable, of the business at particular points in time.

- **Break-even analysis**. Calculates how much product must be sold to pay off the costs of starting and operating the business.

- **Income projections**. Estimates how much money you reasonably expect the business to generate.

- **Cash flow summary**. A summary of money coming into and being paid out of the business.

- **Operating budget summary**. A summary of the expenses needed to run the business.

Formatting and Packaging the Plan

If you are using your business plan only in-house for strategic planning, consider filing it in a three-ring binder. This makes it easy to add new pages and remove sections that become outdated.

If you are presenting your business plan to a banker or a potential investor, have a copy professionally bound at a copy shop or office supply center. Although there are some exceptions, most financiers do not care how creative you are or how revolutionary your designs are. They care about your ability to repay a loan. It is your job to convince them that you are a competent business person. When choosing a cover, lean toward conservative colors, such as black, blue, or dark green.

Make sure that your business plan is easy to read and navigate. Use a standard serif font such as Times New Roman, and include a table of contents.

Using Your Business Plan

Once you have written and formatted your business plan, do not let it see sunlight only when an investor requests a copy. Keep your business plan updated, and refer to it often to compare your business's performance with your pro forma estimates. Recalculate your long-term predictions with the actual sales numbers to identify and prepare for potential financial problems before they become emergencies. Review your marketing plans and consider what strategies have been most successful and which need tweaking.

As you learn more about marketing, business operations, management, and accounting, do not be afraid to revise your business plan. With luck, your business will improve as you gain experience. Your business plan should reflect the improvements.

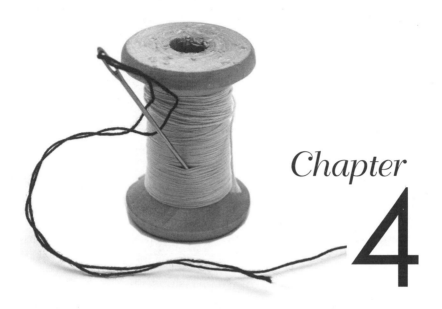

Chapter

4

Developing a Fashion Focus

C hances are you did not decide to start a fashion design business because you were enamored with paperwork, longed to gather financial data, and itched to write a business plan. If you love fashion and the creative process, developing your line might be the most enjoyable part of operating your business.

Before you start sketching, however, it is important to narrow down where you want your business to fit within the industry. Especially when you are just starting your fashion design business, a narrow scope will help you focus on creating high-quality products. If you try to do too much too soon, you may find that you are not creating anything particularly innovative or interesting.

Fashion Genres

There are many divisions in the field of fashion design. Even the largest design houses do not try to cover every genre. A small company may focus on only one or two. Take the time to review the following fashion specialties and consider which ones interest you most as a designer.

Couture

The term haute couture can be used only by companies that meet specific standards in their garment construction and business operations, but "couture" has become synonymous with high-fashion, custom-made formal wear. Couture designs often include unique architecture, lavish fabric, and hand-sewn detailing.

Outerwear

Outerwear includes coats, jackets, headwear, and accessories that people use to stay comfortable in any weather. People need outerwear for special occasions, sports, business, and travel. Outerwear design is a highly specialized field that requires knowledge about how fibers react to different humidity levels and temperatures. Outerwear designers also have to consider how fabrics move and layer over other clothing.

Wedding Gowns

Although couture or formalwear designers may include a white dress or two in their seasonal collections, wedding gowns are a specialty in and of themselves. Modern brides want to express themselves on their special day, and that includes a one-of-a-kind dress.

Not all brides yearn for the traditional, bell-shaped concoction of white satin, gauze, and lace. Some designers offer wedding apparel that reflects the bride's ethnic, religious, or personal background. Others specialize in gowns for plus size, petite, or mature brides.

Sports/Performance Apparel

Casual athletes to elite professionals want clothing that is stylish and attractive. Active apparel is no longer limited to track pants and basketball shorts. Many sports require clothing with practical features. Runners, for example, need shorts with seams that will not cause chafing. Mountain bikers need pants with padding where their legs hit the saddle. Alpine skiers need thin, warm layers they can remove quickly on the trail.

A related type of specialty clothing is dance apparel. Many forms of dance have traditional styles of clothing, but there is always room for improvement or innovation. Scottish dancers need highly embroidered skirts, but an inventive designer may be able to create the required look using moisture-wicking technical fabrics.

Petites

Fashions that look good on a 5-foot-11 model might make someone a foot shorter look dumpy and feel unattractive. Designs for women shorter than 5 feet 4 inches should have different lines and cuts than patterns for taller clients. Simply hemming pants and skirts does not work. Like people of any height, petites need casual clothing, sports apparel, formal wear, business clothes, and accessories.

Plus Size

Just like petites, plus size women and men need clothing that fits their bodies and their life styles. Larger-size clothing may incorporate seaming that accentuates curves and minimizes bulkiness. Certain fabrics add visual weight to clothing and should be avoided.

Children

Contemporary children's fashions can range from cut-down versions of adult styles to nostalgic tunics and bloomers. Parents like to dress their sons and daughters to reflect the family's life style and values. Customers who purchase vegan, ethnic, or religious clothing for themselves look for similar choices for their children. Children involved in pageants, athletics, and dance need targeted clothing and accessories. Families may want coordinated clothes for vacations or special events. Just like adults, children come in many sizes. Age-appropriate clothing for plus size, slim, tall, and petite children is difficult to find in some areas.

Costumes

You do not need to live in a big city to be a professional costume designer. Community theaters, schools, and individuals may need costumes for performances or special events. A talented designer may be able to find a niche creating inventive and unique Halloween costumes.

Historical Wear

People who participate in historical reenactments or who are drawn to a specific time period may want to purchase accurate reproductions of vintage clothing. Vintage-inspired casual or business apparel allows them to wear their interests to the office.

Life Style Wear

Certain life style choices extend into wardrobe selection. People may want apparel associated with specific fetishes, types of music, eating habits, and occupations. Vegans, for example, do not use any animal products. They need clothing and accessories that do not have leather, fur, or wool components. Kitchen workers and medical personnel need sturdy professional clothing that can weather repeated washings in hot water and feature plenty of pockets. Customers concerned with the quality of life in developing countries may require clothing made from materials purchased under fair trade agreements. All these life style choices represent potential fashion design subsets.

Special Needs

People may have physical limitations or special needs that make mainstream clothes impractical. A man with limited fine motor skills may have trouble buttoning a shirt. For a breast-feeding mother, a simple sheath dress presents access problems. Creating adaptive clothing requires more than fashion sense and technical ability. Designers must resolve accessibility issues without compromising their style vision.

Men's Wear

Although their fashions do not change as quickly or remarkably as women's, men also need a range of wardrobe choices that fit their life styles. Men's wear designers might specialize in business attire, formal wear, wedding apparel, or sports clothing.

Accessories

It is a rule of fashion that your client is not fully dressed until he or she is accessorized. A fashion design business may focus entirely on accessories or present them in coordination with their clothing line. There are as many categories of accessories as there are genres of clothing. Athletes need bags to carry their equipment and clothing to the gym or track. Brides need veils and garters. Lace shawls and elegant purses are popular additions to evening wear. In an office, a distinctive briefcase makes a statement. Handbags, belts, wallets, and socks are accessories that people use every day.

Finding Your Niche

In the crowded fashion design industry, it can be difficult for a new business to distinguish itself in one of the broad style categories. Unless you offer something different and exciting, your potential customers, whether they are retail clients or corporate buyers, are likely to purchase from a more established company.

People enjoy dressing to reflect their personality and passions. You can find potential fashion design niches wherever special interests intersect with basic wardrobe needs. If you design and market outerwear, formal attire, accessories, sportswear, or business clothing that reaches any underserved market, the result can be lucrative. The secret is to find that market.

One way to differentiate your designs is to look for overlapping niches with markets that are currently underserved. Snow sports, such as skiing and tubing, for instance, require clothes that are insulated and rugged but are still thin enough to allow the athlete to move. There are many companies that produce stylish and high-quality winter sports clothing. A company that sells vegan or vintage-inspired snow wear may find customers eager to buy their pieces.

Begin brainstorming about potential niches for your business by listing your interests and experiences.

Your Interests

Consider your interests, even those that do not seem directly related to fashion. Whether you enjoy volunteering with an environmental nonprofit organization, playing guitar at the local pub, or walking your dog in the woods, odds are there are other people who like the same things. Think of them as your potential clients. Because you share a hobby, there is already common ground to relate to them.

Your Experiences

Now reflect on your experiences with your hobby, especially as they are related to clothing and accessories. If you often canvas your neighborhood with flyers for your favorite charity, for example, you might want a vest with pockets just the right size to hold standard-size pamphlets. If you are a musician, you might dream of an ethnic-print gig bag. If you are a pet lover, you might enjoy a coat whose pocket has a slit for the leash so you can keep your hands warm while walking your dog.

Unmet Needs

Use the Internet to research what fashion options are available to solve the problems you identified. More important, think of all the different types of people who might have the same problem and determine what markets are underserved. You might find designers who offer utility vests, for example, but all in conservative cuts and colors that would not entice younger customers.

Using the Niche Brainstorming Worksheet

The following worksheet, also found on the CD, can help you organize ideas for finding your market niche.

To complete the worksheet, list your hobbies in the "Interests" circle. If your interests are eclectic, you may find it helpful to group them by related subjects and complete several worksheets. Next, list any needs that you have come across while pursuing your hobbies. Finally, list groups of people who also might have those needs in the "Potential Markets" circle.

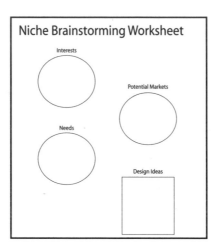

A designer who attends weekly yoga and tribal dance classes, for example, may notice that she is uncomfortably cold at the beginning of class. Other people seem to have the same problem, and several students wear pale pink leg warmers and shrugs they can slip off once their muscles are warmed up. The knitwear clashes with the earth tones of the yoga and dance clothing. When the designer talks to her classmates, she finds that the leg warmers and shrugs are from ballet clothing manufacturers.

The designer might use the information to create the following example worksheet, which helps her determine that there might be a market for leg warmers and shrugs crafted from organic fiber and coordinated with the kind of apparel she sees students wear to yoga and tribal dance classes.

Expanding Your Niche

Once you have determined a need and a potential market, it is all right to think bigger. The initial niche you define does not have to be the end target for your endeavor. Unless it is your dream to design those particular articles, think of them as a stepping stone toward advancing your fashion business.

A designer who starts by creating accessories for tennis players, for example, may decide to expand into tennis outfits and training clothing after gaining name recognition within the market.

On the other hand, if you enjoy designing for the niche you have carved out for your business and find success in the market, there is nothing wrong with specializing in one particular product. Fashion is a dynamic, constantly changing industry, and there are ample opportunities to experiment with new techniques, patterns, and materials. Even designing within a narrow scope can remain challenging and fun.

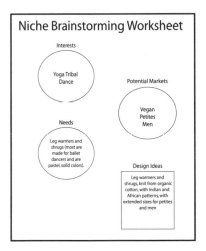

Finding Inspiration

After you decide on a niche for your business, you can start focusing your designs. One way to develop a cohesive line is to create apparel based on a common source of inspiration.

You can find inspiration anywhere. Look for places, objects, or events that are rich in texture, color, shapes, or patterns. You may find the perfect piece in your environment. Nature is full of potential sources. Your seasonal collection could draw from the palette of forest colors in autumn or the textural pattern of a snake's skin. You could base an entire line on the gentle curve and subtle color variations on a single daffodil petal. The environment also includes man-made elements. The lines of a skyscraper, the textures on a brick wall, and the colors on a mural might inspire you.

Inspiration may come from past fashions, architecture, and technology. You might design your clothes based on the practical women's separates from World War II or the light, feminine offerings found a few years later. The clean, organic lines of prairie-style buildings might lend themselves to the silhouettes of your wedding dresses. You might find an antique lamp, table, or toy that calls to you. The delicate weathering and aged colors could provide a basis for your designs.

Textiles from other cultures are common sources of design inspiration. You can pull a single motif or a selection of colors from a woven blanket to use as a unifying element in your line. You can gather spices, fibers, photographs, and artwork from a single location and look for common colors, textures, and patterns to sprinkle throughout your pieces.

You may draw your inspiration from current trends. The pieces you design today may not be seen in stores for another year or 18 months. By then, your looks may seem outdated. Instead of looking at your local department and specialty stores for inspiration, check out how people are modifying their clothing. Pay special attention to groups that seem to be a trend or two ahead of your target market.

Creating a Storyboard

Designers use storyboards to show the elements that inspire a particular line. Your storyboard is a collage that helps you organize these elements, see new connections between them, and present them to other people.

The first step toward creating a storyboard is to gather items that represent your inspiration. If your designs will be based around a piece of cloth, photograph, or small item, this is a straightforward step. However, if your inspiration is less tangible, for example a sun setting over a mountain range, you may need to be more creative in what you include. You may want to collect a picture of your inspiration or even several pictures from different angles.

Now collect other materials that support your inspiration. Make sample swatches using paints, fabrics, or fibers that capture the colors of your inspirational moment. Be sure to make several samples of each so you can play with how the elements interact together. Sketch out a few rough silhouettes based on the lines of your source. Look for other objects that echo any textural components. Find anything that reminds you of your inspiration in some way.

Once you have gathered plenty of swatches, images, and objects, lay them all out on your worktable and start playing. Give yourself plenty of time to see what works together and what should be weeded out. Just because something is not directly connected to your inspiration does not mean it should not be included on your storyboard. However, everything you do include should have a progression from your inspiration. For example, if your line will be built around an heirloom quilt with a gray background, you might find some pebbles that are the same shade of gray. The texture of the pebbles might connect a series of fabrics and colors not found on the original inspiration piece.

File away any materials not connected to your original inspiration or that do not work together with the other elements. Be sure not to throw these pieces away. You might later decide they do belong on your storyboard, or you may want to use them with another collection.

When you have decided what you will include on your storyboard, find a suitable mounting board and start working with different arrangements and layouts. Mounting boards come in a variety of sizes, colors, and materials. When choosing a mounting board, keep in mind where you plan on taking your storyboard, how you will display it, and the number, colors, sizes, and weights of the elements it is to hold. Mounting boards made by sandwiching a thick foam core between two sheets of paper are often a good choice, as they are sturdy and easy to cut and drill. You can display a foam board by leaning it against a wall or on an easel.

Storyboard Layouts

Once you have selected the elements you are displaying, it is time to organize the components to tell the inspiration story of your line or design.

The layout you choose depends on the type and number of elements you are going to include. If you have one large inspiration piece and many supporting swatches, you can mount the inspiration piece near the center of the board and encircle it with swatches that directly connect to it. In an outer circle, arrange pieces that have a secondary relationship to the inspiration piece. To create a cohesive storyboard, place secondary swatches near the element that ties them to the inspiration piece.

If you have several connected inspiration pieces, mount them on the board with connecting swatches, creating a flow between the inspiration pieces.

If you have a single inspiration piece with only a few supporting swatches or if you are presenting a completed design, consider a clean layout with the inspiration piece or final drawing on one side and supporting swatches on the other.

If you drew your ideas from many elements instead of a central inspiration, a free-form collage might be the most complete way to represent your line. Diagrams for each of these storyboard layouts are on the accompanying CD.

As you experiment with different layouts, you might want to use temporary adhesive putty to keep each element in position. Once you are sure of your layout and the positioning of each element, it is time to permanently attach the pieces to the storyboard. Some mounting boards are self-adhesive, but others will need a type of glue to attach storyboard elements. Before you use any adhesive, test it on a small piece of the swatch, picture, or object you are going to affix. Make sure the glue does not cause any damage or discoloration. You may need several varieties of glue for a single storyboard.

Using a Storyboard

If you constructed a storyboard to show the inspiration behind a work in progress, keep the board handy to refer to whenever you work on the line or design. Take it with you to suppliers to make sure any fabric, fiber, trim, or accessories you purchase are the right colors and textures. Do not trust your memory. Hold swatches up to your storyboard to make sure they are compatible with the inspirational elements.

Be aware that colors and patterns can appear differently under natural versus artificial light. In dim warehouses or storage areas, it can be hard to tell what coordinates and what clashes. Do not be afraid to ask to take a bolt of cloth outside to compare it to the samples on your storyboard. Alternatively, carry a small flashlight with you so you can analyze supplies on the spot.

Never assume that all units grouped together on a shelf or in a bin are the same color. Even subtle color mistakes can stand out on and detract from a finished garment. Check and double-check every component before you buy. Keep your receipts in case you need to return items because of color imperfections.

If you are using the storyboard to present a design or line to clients, take extra care to keep it pristine. To limit damage from moving or storing the board, attach a protective cover that can be removed or flipped to the back so that potential customers can touch swatches and evaluate textures. Consider making a separate, portable storyboard to take with you on shopping trips or to use in the workroom.

CASE STUDY: PRIMARY PRACTICAL KNITS

Kelly Feibes, Owner
Primarily Practical Knits
Lexington, Kentucky
www.primarilypracticalknits.com

I love knits, but I noticed that most commercially available knits are either luxury items or cheaply made. Cheap knits do not look good for long, and they fall apart quickly. Luxury knits are too expensive for many families and are not always high quality.

I decided to provide knitwear that will meet the typical family's needs. I use quality yarns that last for years but avoid expensive yarns that require special handling. I finish each item by hand to guarantee that it will not unravel in the wash.

Primarily Practical Knits was registered as a limited liability corporation in July 2003. I maintain complete control over every item so that I feel comfortable guaranteeing the quality of my products.

My advice for new designers is to be flexible. Do your research, think things through carefully, and start your business with the best-laid plans possible. Be aware that the direction of your business might change dramatically after the first year. This is all good and part of the fun.

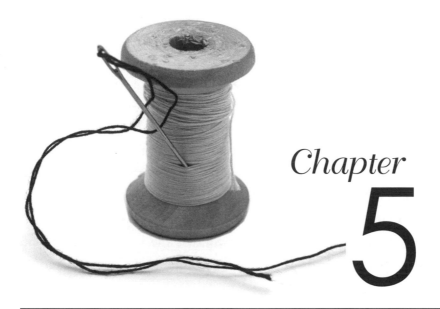

Chapter

5

Designing Your Line

Design Basics

ecoming a good designer requires study, practice, and experimentation. You need to look at your work and the work of other designers with a critical eye to get a feel for what works. You may need to sketch dozens of ideas before you find a look you want to pursue. Do not be afraid to try new ideas or arrange traditional concepts in fresh ways.

Fashion design can be framed into 11 principles: line, form, rhythm, balance, proportion, focal point, color, texture, hand, unity, and contrast. You should consider each principle by itself and as part of the entire garment when editing your designs.

Line

Line refers to the silhouette of a design. If you are evaluating the line of an existing garment, consider how it would look in two dimensions and then trace the outside edges created by the fabric. In this way, complex fashion can often be reduced to a simple geometric shape such as a triangle, oval, rectangle, or a combination of two or three shapes. When someone wears a garment, his or her body, in addition to the cut and seaming, may influence the line of material. If you desire a garment with a rigid line, as opposed to a flow that follows the model's curves, you need to use a firm fabric or use structural components, such as padding or boning.

Form

The line creates the form of the garment. The form of a garment encompasses how much space it occupies in three dimensions, whereas line describes the garment in two dimensions. The form of a piece of clothing can be hard to describe with a single sketch, so designers may draw the garment from several angles. This is especially important if the garment has complicated form elements, such as bellows or ruffles.

Rhythm

The pattern of the fabric you choose and the placement of details across the garment help guide the viewer's eye. For example, thick diagonal stripes that begin at the shoulders and converge at the waist draw attention to the midline. The way people look across a piece, where they linger, and what parts they skip, create the rhythm of the outfit.

Balance

How the patterns, graphics, details, and trim are positioned on the garment also help determine the visual weight of the design. Balance describes how evenly the visual weight is distributed. Most fashion designs are balanced from left to right; however, this does not mean they are symmetrical in every way. Different elements can provide similar visual weight and balance each other. Consider an asymmetric sleeveless shirt that is designed to be worn off the shoulder on one side. A lower or detailed hem on the same side as the bare shoulder could provide enough visual weight to make the design balanced and attractive.

Depending on the style, balance from top to bottom can be even or uneven. Evenly balanced designs have the same visual weight above the waist as they do below. This can be achieved by using the same patterns in the same proportions. An unevenly balanced design can be achieved by using smaller amounts of more vivid elements. A leopard-print blouse, for example, may be balanced by a neutral skirt.

Proportion

Balance is closely related to proportion. Where balance refers to the visual weight of a garment, proportion refers to the relative size of the component pieces. Small and large pieces can be combined for effective designs: for example, a voluminous skirt paired with a fitted shirt.

Focal Point

Embroidery at the neckline of a blouse, a wild graphic on a casual T-shirt, and industrial-inspired buckles on a formal pump are all details that catch viewers' attention and encourage them to look longer. These details are the focal points of the garments — elements that are emphasized. You can create a focal point with cut, seams, trim, graphics, or other elements. A focal point is a single design feature.

Color

When selecting a color scheme for your design, consider both the tone and the value of your options. Colors in close proximity influence each other, so be sure to experiment with swatches before committing to any fabric or trim. A book or course in color theory can help you learn how to use the color wheel to develop effective color combinations.

Texture

Texture refers to the surface quality of the garment. The texture of a fabric is the result of the fibers and the technique used to weave or knit the fabric. A subtle texture may not be obvious to viewers unless they are close, but the right texture can be the difference between a design that works and one that potential customers pass by. Textures can be difficult to show on a sketch, so consider attaching a swatch of fabric if the texture is an important feature in a design.

Hand

Clothing can be stiff and rigid or flexible and fluid. The hand of a garment is a description of how it drapes and flows when touched. Texture refers to the surface of the material, but hand takes into consideration the weight and thickness of the fabric, as well as the fibers used and the tightness of the weave. The hand of the fabric you choose will help determine how the garment hangs and how seams and trimmings sit.

Unity

The unity of a design refers to the connection between the different pieces of the garment. One way to create unity in your design is through repetition. Nearly any design element can be repeated. You can use the same line or form in a shirt as in a skirt. Even in different proportions, the result can be unifying. You can repeat patterns, textures, and colors throughout a piece. Unity helps create the sense that a design is intentional.

Contrast

Contrasting colors, textures, proportions, lines, forms, and hands can add interest to your design. A slice of white on black skirt can serve as a focal point, or it can be a unifying element between the skirt and a white blouse. The more different elements are, the more intense the contrasting effect. A blue stripe at the hem of a turquoise shirt can leave the viewer wondering if there had been a piecing or dyeing mistake. The same blue stripe on a red shirt is an obvious contrasting element.

Sketching Your Ideas

Making the design elements work together can be a complicated process. Few designers are able to create good fashion without editing and reworking their ideas. Design drawings are a useful way to see how different components work together and to try out new looks. If you create custom fashions for your clients, a quick sketch can help you communicate your vision and clarify what the customer wants.

In a traditional fashion educational program, figure drawing is taught in addition to garment construction and design. Not only does learning how to draw the human body help designers understand anatomy and proportion, but professional-looking fashion drawings can be used instead of photographs to promote completed designs in marketing publications and Web pages.

Fashion drawings have a different proportion than realistic drawings. In nature, the length of an average human body is seven and one half times the length of the head. In fashion drawings, this proportion is increased to eight and a half. The added length is the result of an elongation of the leg. This helps show fashions to their best advantage.

There are three main types of fashion drawings. Working drawings are used to show the details of a garment's construction to the pattern cutter. Quick poses are used to show ideas to clients or collaborators. Finished drawings are used for presentations or publications. They show the style, line, and texture of the outfit and should be congruent with the designer company's image.

Fashion photographs are a good source of practice material for sketches. Copying the photographs can help you learn some common modeling poses and typical fabric movement. Until you are proficient at sketching, use a template to trace a figure when you need to experiment with different fashion ideas.

Matching Materials to Intended Use

Early in the design process, you should consider what type of material you plan to use to make each sketch a reality. Understanding the properties of the materials you use is essential for any fashion designer. Often several types of fibers and styles of fabric will work with a single design. This is a cost-effective way of filling out your line, as the pattern and manufacturing process will not change significantly.

Types of Fibers

There are two major categories of fibers: man-made and natural.

Man-made fibers can be made out of cellulose or petroleum. Rayon is a cellulose-based fiber. Nylon is a petroleum product. Regenerated cellulose-based fibers are made from dissolved and extruded wood pulp. Petroleum-based fibers are also called synthetic fibers.

Natural fibers can come from animals or plants. Animal fibers such as wool, mohair, and alpaca are good insulators because the lofty filaments do not pack against each other. Plant fibers such as hemp and cotton tend to absorb large amounts of water, making them good choices for clothing worn in warm conditions. Natural fibers may be treated to change their original properties. For example, wool can be treated so that it does not felt when it is washed in warm water.

Natural and man-made fibers can be used together to created blended fibers and fabrics that combine the characteristics of their components. An example is adding a small amount of spandex to cotton, which gives some elasticity to the relatively brittle natural fiber. Garments made out of the blended fabric will keep their shape better than those made out of pure cotton but remain appealing to consumers who prefer the look and feel of natural fibers.

Commonly Used Fibers

A key step to creating a well-thought-out design is determining the right fiber to use. A design that looks beautiful with a fluid, draping silk might not work with a stiff cotton. A pair of structured trousers, on the other hand, might look better with crisp cotton or linen. Even within the same fiber family, different types of spinning, weaving, or knitting produce fabric with different properties.

The following chart, which is also found on the accompanying CD, summarizes the properties of some of the most popular fiber families.

PROPERTIES OF COMMON FIBERS						
Fiber	Water Management	Insulating	Softness	Wrinkling	Drape	Strength
Cotton	Absorbent	No	Soft	Heavy	Poor drape	Strong
Linen	Absorbent	No	Soft	Heavy	Fair drape	Strong
Ramie	Absorbent	No	Soft	Heavy	Fair drape	Strong
Silk	Absorbent	Yes	Soft	Heavy	Good drape	Strong
Wool	Absorbent	Yes	Depends on weave	Depends on weave	Good drape	Weak
Acetate	Not absorbent	No	Soft	Light	Good drape	Weak
Nylon	Not absorbent	No	Depends on weave	Light	Depends on weave	Strong
Acrylic	Absorbent	Yes	Soft	Light	Depends on weave	Strong
Polyester	Not absorbent	Yes	Depends on weave	Light	Depends on weave	Strong
Rayon	Absorbent	No	Soft	Heavy	Good Drape	Strong

Common Natural Fabrics

Fibers are woven or knit to create fabrics, which differ in appearance, care requirements, durability, drape, and texture. Fabrics can be classified according to fiber families.

Silk

Silkworm cocoons are harvested for silk fiber, which is used to weave a variety of fabrics. Some common silk fabrics that you may want to incorporate into your designs include:

- **China silk:** Plain weave, smooth silk fabric with a high luster

- **Douppioni:** Fabric woven from uneven silk threads

- **Faille:** Glossy, ribbed silk

- **Georgette:** Crinkled, sheer crepe

- **Matelassé:** Silk fibers woven with raised designs

- **Noil:** A soft fabric made of short silk fibers

- **Organza:** Thin, transparent silk

- **Peau de Soie or paduasoy:** Crisp fabric with thin cross ribs and corded appearance

- **Pongee:** A thin silk with a rough texture

- **Silk linen:** Plain weave silk with nubby crosshatches in both directions

Linen

Linen is woven from flax fiber, which is exceptionally strong and absorbent. The most common linen fabrics are:

- **Butcher linen:** A heavy, canvas-like weave

- **Damask:** Plain or satin weave linen with a raised pattern

- **Venise:** Damask linen featuring a floral pattern and made out of fine threads

Cotton

Cotton is a popular fiber because of its versatility. Cotton can be woven or knit by itself or blended with other fibers to be used in casual clothing, formal wear, or couture creations. The most common include:

- **Duck:** Tightly woven canvas

- **Muslin:** Plain weave cotton of any thickness

- **Organdy:** Thin, transparent weave

- **Poplin:** Woven cotton with a small side-to-side rib

- **Sateen:** Satin weave cotton

- **Terry cloth**: Heavily piled, absorbent cotton

Animal Fibers

Because of the serrated texture of the individual fibers, animal hair such as alpaca, angora, mohair, sheep's wool, and camel hair can be woven, knit, or even pressed numerous ways. Animal fiber uses include:

- **Broadcloth:** Woven fabric in a slight nap

- **Challis:** Light fabric woven to include a floral design

- **Donegal:** Woven tweed with thick slubs

- **Felt:** Compressed mat of fibers

- **Flannel:** Lightweight weave with a moderate nap

- **Gabardine:** Tightly woven twill

- **Jersey:** Lightweight knit of fine fibers

- **Mackinaw:** Heavy fabric with reversible, colored pattern

- **Oatmeal cloth:** Soft weave with a bumpy texture

- **Tartan:** Woven plaid

- **Tweed:** Thick, rough weave

Performance Fabrics

"Technical" or "performance" fibers and fabrics are created out of synthetic fibers or natural/synthetic fiber blends. These fabrics may be knit or woven to bring out specific qualities, usually related to heat or water management, of the fiber. Coolmax® from Invista is a family of technical fabrics that wick away perspiration and help wearers feel cool even in hot weather. Other technical fibers have increased insulating or water-repelling properties.

Like Coolmax®, most performance fibers and fabrics are trademarked products. Technical fibers are often slight variants of generic synthetic fibers. Lycra®, a registered trademark of Invista, for example, is a derivative of spandex developed by DuPont. Brand-name fibers are more expensive than their parent fibers.

Chemical companies invest time and money to develop and market technical fibers and fabrics. Just like designers who try to create an image that will appear to the target market of their apparel, chemical companies develop campaigns to brand their merchandise to appeal to athletes, the environmentally conscious, parents, hunters, students, or other populations.

To protect this image, the trademark holder may impose stringent guidelines regarding the use of the branded fiber, fabric, logo, motto, or name. If you decide to use a branded technical fabric on your designs, expect some limitations.

Fiber Identification Process

Because of Federal Trade Commission labeling regulations, you may not be able to sell garments unless you are certain of the source and kind of fiber used in their manufacture. However, you may find that the unlabeled remnant of fabric you grabbed out of the bargain bin works perfectly on one of your test garments. In that case, the ability to make a tentative identification of this fabric can help you narrow down what type of fiber you want to use to produce the garments you sell. By limiting the fabric you have to purchase for experiments and the number of additional test garments you have to prepare, being able to identify fibers can save money and time.

The burn test is a handy way to narrow down fiber used to make a sample of fabric. Because you are working with fire and possibly flammable materials, be sure to have a fire extinguisher handy when performing these tests. The following worksheet detailing the burn test for fiber identification is also on the accompanying CD.

The burn test does have limitations. It is not easy to distinguish between different animal fibers, such as wool or alpaca, or between plant fibers, such as hemp and cotton. Also, blends can give conflicting or inaccurate results. However, it is a good starting point for identifying a mystery fabric.

Fiber Identification Worksheet

Note: Be sure to have a fire extinguisher handy when performing these tests.

1. **Cut a small sample of the fiber.** Using a pair of tweezers, hold the sample over a bowl of water. Light a long match and bring the flame to the edge of the fiber sample.

   - The fiber flames and burns quickly. Possibilities include acrylic, acetate, and plant fibers (such as flax, cotton, or hemp).

   - The fiber burns slowly. Possibilities include polyester and olefin.

   - The fiber melts away from the flame and continues to burn slowly. Possibilities include silk and animal fibers (such as wool, cashmere, or alpaca).

2. **Remove the fiber from the flame.**

   - The fiber extinguishes but continues to melt. Possibilities include acrylic, olefin, nylon, or polyester.

   - The fiber burns and melts. Possibilities include acetate.

↳ The fiber extinguishes. Possibilities include silk and animal fibers.

↳ The fiber glows. Possibilities include plant fibers.

3. **Which best describes the ashes from the burnt fiber?**

↳ Hard and black. Possibilities include acetate, acrylic, and polyester.

↳ Hard and gray. Possibilities include nylon.

↳ Hard and brown. Possibilities include olefin.

↳ Soft and black. Possibilities include animal fibers, silk, and mercerized cotton.

↳ Soft and gray. Possibilities include cotton, hemp, jute, and linen.

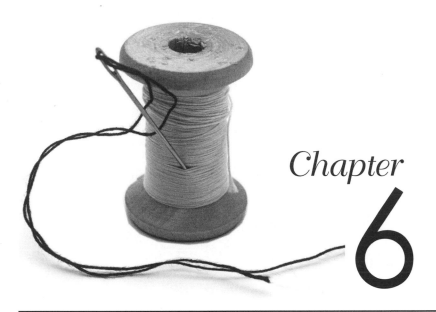

Chapter

6

Sample Garments

Once you have completed your design and chosen the fabrics, you are ready to construct the first sample.

Sample garments have an important role in the fashion industry. They allow you to see your design on a model. Once you see the garment moving in three dimensions, you might decide it needs more editing or should be cut from the line entirely. The process of manufacturing the sample garment will also help you estimate the expense of producing that design. Bulk production of a design is often about one-third to one-half the cost of producing the sample.

Completed sample garments can be useful marketing tools. You can show them to buyers at fashion marts, trunk shows, or in-store demonstrations. Professional photographs of your line, when displayed on your Web site or print materials, can help build your image.

Patternmaking

To construct a sample, you will need a pattern from which to cut material. If you are skilled at patternmaking, drafting your own can save you significant time and money. If you hire a patternmaker, you might lose time by having to redo the pattern if he or she did not understand the design thoroughly and made a mistake. You also have to work around the time constraints and schedule of the patternmaker, which can leave you waiting weeks or even months for the completed patterns.

Designers who draft their own patterns have another opportunity to fix problems or edit a look before the sample garments are constructed. If you lack the technical skills to draft your own patterns, consider taking a course in patternmaking or draping. Until you are proficient, hire a professional.

If you hire a patternmaker, confirm that he or she has time for your project. Be sure to get an estimate for the cost. Some patternmakers charge by the hour; others charge by the piece. Get the deposit and editing policy in writing.

Patternmakers may specialize in certain types of garments. Choose a contractor who has experience making the kind of clothing you design. The patternmaker will need to know everything about the look, including the widths and lengths of the components (including pockets and sleeves), detailing, and the fabric you plan to use. Your designs are your creative property. The patternmaker you choose should have a privacy policy to protect your work.

Basic Construction Skills

Designers who are skilled sewers can save money by constructing samples themselves. Your samples will be your calling cards to buyers. If you cannot do a professional job, hire a contractor who will make your clothes look as nice as possible.

Small-scale custom designers may find it faster and easier to do their own sewing. Even if you intend to hire a seamstress or tailor, by understanding construction and sewing basics you will be better able to communicate with manufacturers and recognize poor work.

Fashion designers should be able to:

- Differentiate between common types of seams

- Understand what seams work better for different fabrics, garments, and looks

- Set sleeves

- Understand the function and placement of facings, interfacings, and linings

- Insert zippers, snaps, and buttons

- Fit collars, lapels, and pockets

- Hem edges

If you are not a proficient sewer, consider taking classes from your local design school, craft store, or sewing machine dealer. Seamstresses and tailors sometimes offer private lessons.

Sewing Equipment

If you do not plan on sewing your own samples or garments, you may use a home sewing machine for experimentation and alterations. Home machines, even if they are labeled "semi-industrial" or "industrial strength," have substantially less power than industrial machines. Most industrial sewing machines have about half-horsepower (hp) motors and are capable of sewing more than 4,500 stitches per minute (spm). Home machines, on the other hand, usually top out at 1/10 hp and 800 spm.

Home machines are often much cheaper than industrial machines. They also tend to sew less consistent stitches. Where industrial machines usually make only one type of stitch, basic home machines might produce dozens of different stitch patterns. Because industrial sewing machines are so specialized, production workrooms will have several different machines.

Types of industrial sewing machines include:

- **Drop feed:** Sews a straight stitch through lightweight to medium weight fabrics

- **Needle feed:** Sews a straight stitch through heavier fabrics

- **Walking foot:** Sews a straight stitch through thick or heavy fabrics

- **Zig-zag:** Allows for side-to-side motion in addition to straight stitch

- **Blind stitch:** Makes a stitch that cannot be seen on the right side of the fabric, used for linings and cuffs

- **Serger or overlock:** Creates finished, trimmed seams. Comes in different formations for different types of material and garments

Hiring a Seamstress or Tailor

Because there is a high initial investment in professional equipment and training, hiring someone to construct your samples may be less expensive. Depending on the types of garments you design, your location, the number of samples you need, and the length of time you are able to wait for your samples, you may decide to have your samples sewn by a freelance sewer or by a clothing factory.

When interviewing people to sew your samples, keep in mind the following questions:

- Do they have the skills needed to complete the job? Working with special material such as leather or fur is different than working with cotton fabric.

- Do they have experience making that type of garment?

- Do they understand the special techniques required to construct the garment?

- What training have they received?

- Will they adjust the garment if it is not right?

- Do they have the equipment needed to make the garment look perfect?

- How long will it take for them to complete the garment?

Sewers can give valuable advice about construction techniques. Listen to their input about what hems, seams, and fasteners work with your chosen fabrics and cuts. They may offer suggestions for better ways to get the same effects.

When using professional sewers, do not put them in the position of being the designer. They will not get any credit if an idea works, and it is not fair to blame them if a suggestion ruins a look.

Be sure to get several estimates before committing to a contractor. Although the cheapest option is not always the best, talking with several sewers will help you understand more about the industry and make a more informed decision about the going rate of the service.

Contractors may be limited by the material you give them to work with. Check for damage and inconsistencies before you leave supplies with the sewers. Have them inspect the materials, too, and sign an inspection sheet noting any problems.

Signs of a High-Quality Garment

Before you accept a completed sample garment from a contractor, look it over carefully to make sure that is well sewn and fitted. Seams should lay smooth and have even stitching. Make sure any fasteners are secure. The fabric grain line of each part of the garment should match what was indicated in the pattern. Buttonholes should be neat and finished. If the garment is made out of patterned fabric, the pattern should match up across the parts of the garment and be centered appropriately on the front. Hemlines should be even and clean. Check to make sure the material has not been damaged by pressing and loose threads are trimmed.

If there are any metal or plastic details on the piece, make sure they are securely attached and free of burrs. There should not be any visible glue residue. Leather pieces should be of even thickness and finish. Trim should be sewn neatly and evenly, with smooth overlaps.

Have your fit model try on the garments so you can see if any alterations are needed.

Look over anything you sew with the same critical eye. Noticing mistakes will help you prevent them in the future.

Grading

If you decide, after seeing the sample, that a look works and deserves a place in your line, you may have to get additional patterns made that adjust the garment to fit on different size bodies. Accessories and some clothing may be "one size fits most."

Grading, or sizing, the pattern up and down, is a precision process. Unless you are trained and experienced, hire a professional. Your patternmaker or sewing contractor might be able to recommend a competent local grader. Some online services are also available.

Legal Considerations

The works you create are a kind of property. As a designer, you have certain rights to that property. You also have the responsibility not to infringe on the property rights of other people.

The fashion design industry is filled with legal and ethical dilemmas: Can you use another designer's line for inspiration? How much do you have to change a pattern to call it your own design? What images and patterns can you use in your designs? How can you protect your designs from being copied?

Protecting Your Creative Property

You have invested months in researching, sketching, and sewing your prototypes. Within weeks, an unethical manufacturer can copy your designs and have them in retail stores under his or her label. To protect your creative property and your business, you need to understand your legal rights.

A copyright refers to the property rights to an original creative work. The owner of a copyright can publish, reproduce, and sell the work. A piece is automatically protected by a copyright from the moment it is created until 70 years after the creator's death.

Garment styles are not protected by copyright laws. However, any original textile prints and graphics you create for your designs are protected. Although copyrights are effective as soon as a work is created, you may need to register your copyright to bring legal proceedings for copyright infringement. You can register copyrights through the United States Copyright Office:

> U.S. Copyright Office
> 101 Independence Avenue SE
> Washington, D.C. 20559-6000
> 202-707-5959
> **www.copyright.gov**

If you develop a new and innovative process for creating your fashions, you can apply for a patent through the United States Patent and Trademark Office. Garment designs cannot be patented.

A trademark is a word, name, symbol, or device used to distinguish a product from similar items. A product or process itself is not trademarked. The name, logo, or slogan that identifies the product is the trademark. You can register a trademark for ten years. After that, it can be renewed as long as it remains in use. Generic words such as "great" and "jacket" cannot be trademarked. If a trademarked word becomes synonymous with the generic product or process, the registration renewal may be denied.

"Trade dress" refers to the look of a product or its packaging that distinguishes and identifies the product, such as the distinctive blue box used by Tiffany & Co. Although trade dress infringement may be more difficult to prove than trademark infringement, designers have successfully used this concept to stop other people from making copies of their creations.

You can apply for patents and register trademarks through the United States Patent and Trademark Office:

> United States Patent and Trademark Office
> PO Box 1450
> Alexandria, VA 22313-1450
> 1-800-786-9199
> **www.uspto.gov**

Copying Designs

Re-creating all or part of another designer's work not only exposes you to possible legal action, but it may ruin your reputation in the fashion industry. In addition, if your garments are strikingly similar to others on the market, you lose the ability to position yourself as innovative or unique.

Using and Altering Patterns

Using a simple commercial pattern as a template for your design may be acceptable. After all, there are only so many ways to cut an A-line skirt or T-shirt. The pattern you use should be only a starting point. The finished garment should not look as if it came from the pattern and should require a new pattern to reproduce.

Some alterations you may wish to perform on a pattern include:

- Raise or lower the hem

- Add, remove, or move pockets

- Change sleeve shape or length

- Increase or decrease volume

- Add vents, pleats, or darts

- Include structural elements

- Reshape the neckline

- Change the shoulder attachment

- Add trim or details

If you are in doubt about using an existing pattern, consult an attorney who specializes in intellectual property.

Licensed Images and Phrases

If your designs feature an image, name, logo, or pattern associated with another label, an entertainer, a fictional character, a celebrity, a company, a team, an event, or another past or present entity, you may need to buy the legal rights to use the intellectual material.

When you enter a licensing agreement, you are given certain rights in exchange for payment. Payment may be in the form of royalties on the wholesale price of the garments that will feature the licensed property.

If you use licensed material, expect to give up some design freedom to support the brand of the licensor. As the licensee, you may be required to use certain colors in your design, to reproduce the licensed image only at specific sizes, and to market your garments through retail establishments of a certain caliber. For example, a celebrity may not want her picture on shirts sold through discount chains.

Make sure you have a signed contract with the legal copyright holders before you use any image, name, phrase, or pattern you did not come up with yourself. Your licensing agreement should address:

- **Time limits**. How long will you be licensed to use the intellectual property?

- **Cost**. How much will you be required to pay in royalties? The industry standard ranges from 7 to 14 percent of the wholesale price. When will payments be due? Will you need to pay an advance on the royalties? Is there a guaranteed minimum you will have to pay regardless of the number of items you sell?

- **Marketing limits**. How will you be able to market your products? What methods are unacceptable? How will the agreement change if you market your products in an unacceptable way?

- **Distribution**. Where will you be allowed to sell your products? Will there be a minimum price per garment? Are online sales allowed?

- **Design limits**. From what kind of material will you need to manufacture your garments? What design features will be required or forbidden?

- **Quality**. Will you have to submit to quality testing from the licensor? If so, how often and by whom will the tests be performed?

Because licensing agreements can be so restrictive, you may be tempted to skip the process and use a copyrighted element anyway or change the property just slightly. If you do this, not only are you risking potential legal troubles, but you are sabotaging other people who make their living through their creativity. Artists and writers put as much work into their copyrighted images and phrases as designers invest in their fashions.

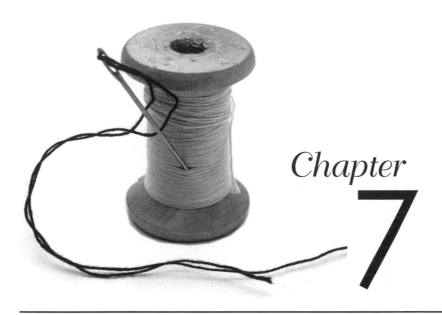

Selling Your Designs

B y the time you have your designs and samples, you may have spent a sizeable portion of your business budget in addition to hours of labor and research. The good news is that now you can start marketing your designs and trying to bring money into your business through sales.

Retail Options

By selling your apparel directly to the end user, you decide how to display, price, and market each piece. There are several ways fashion design business owners can retail their clothes.

Trunk Shows

Trunk shows can be one of the easiest and least expensive ways to reach retail customers. When you hold a trunk show, you display your entire line to a group of potential customers. The attendees can place orders for styles they like. One of the major benefits of a trunk show is that you do not have to invest in a large amount of standing inventory in various sizes. You can hold a trunk show using your samples, but be sure to have firm quotes from manufacturers before you take any orders. You do not want to price your clothing too low to pay for the construction costs.

Several types of venues are suitable for a trunk show. You may hold one in a retail space, such as a clothing store or accessories boutique. If you plan on wholesaling to a particular store, an after-hours trunk show can help you and the owners see how the customers respond to your designs.

If you have current customers who are enthusiastic about your clothing, they may be willing to host trunk shows in their home. It is common to extend a percentage of the evening's sales or credit toward future purchases to the hosts of private showings.

You may prefer to hold a trunk show in your own studio. Customers may enjoy an inside view of the design process. If you sew your own clothing, you can demonstrate any special techniques or materials you use.

You may be able to rent a common area, such as a meeting hall, a section of a retail mall, or a shelter at a park, to display your apparel. If you go this route, look for a location that is frequented by members of your target market, and choose a time when there will be of foot traffic.

Before holding a trunk show, make sure you have a signed contract with the host. The contract should address exactly where and at what time the trunk show will be, when it will end, the percentage of net sales the host is entitled to, and any fees involved. In addition, make sure both parties understand their responsibilities, including:

- Who will provide models?

- Who will set up the venue?

- Who is in charge of cleaning up after the show?

- What kind of marketing will you each provide?

- What kind of refreshments will be provided? Who will be responsible for arranging and paying for the refreshments?

- Will additional lighting be needed? If so, who will provide it?

Before the trunk show, make sure all your samples are clean, repaired, pressed, and stored to prevent wrinkles and damage. If you will be using models, get their sizes so your samples can be altered if needed. If you will not be using models, make sure that there will be appropriate mannequins or dress forms to display your apparel. Prepare marketing materials that promote your line and your business. Have plenty of order forms, business cards, and pens on hand.

Prepare a note card for each piece in your collection. On it, list the construction features, materials used, price, and sizes available. If other colors or variations are available for order, list those as well and prepare swatch books for the customers to review. Be prepared to talk about the inspiration behind each piece and what sets it apart from similar styles.

Give customers an honest estimate of how long they will have to wait for their orders. Make sure the clothes you show will arrive in plenty of time for the appropriate wearing season.

Use the following checklist, also found on the accompanying CD, to help organize your trunk show.

	TRUNK SHOW CHECKLIST
	Negotiate and sign a contract with the host.
	Organize event marketing, including newspaper advertisements, direct mail pieces, flyers, and radio spots.
	Contract models.
	Measure models.
	Assign pieces to models.
	Fit samples to models.
	List what samples need repairs or alterations.
	Send samples, with a detailed list, to seamstress. Specify that alterations should be reversible.
	Fit altered samples to models.
	Review samples. Press and store them when satisfied with alterations and repairs.
	Design venue decorations. Remember to plan guest seating.
	Prepare sample notes.
	Prepare order forms.
	Gather marketing supplies, including promotional look books, brochures, catalogs, and business cards.
	Schedule a "day of" run-through with the models.
	Organize refreshments.
	Write a schedule for the event.
	Arrange a cleanup crew to help after the show.
	Decorate the venue.
	Bring pens and order forms.
	Clean up.
	Tally sales and pay the host.
	Write a thank-you note to the host.
	Manufacture and ship orders. Include marketing materials for follow-up sales.

Designer-Owned Boutiques

You may decide to sell your apparel through your own boutique. This can be a profitable option for designers who know there is a local market for their clothing and can afford to operate a retail shop and a fashion business.

There are several ways you can incorporate a retail store and fashion design. Your store may be the only source of your clothing, or you may also supply to other retailers. You can have a store that sells apparel only from your label, or you may sell other fashions, accessories, and gifts that coordinate with your clothes or appeal to your target market.

Your storefront may be permanent, seasonal, or transient. Permanent storefronts operate from one place year round. Seasonal stores are open only during specific sale periods, such as the winter holidays or summer tourist season. Transient stores are temporary structures that can be set up at fairs, trade shows, or other short-term events.

No matter which type of storefront you choose, the location of your retail shop is a major factor in your profitability. A good store location is one that is convenient and popular with your target market. Look for a space that is large enough to show off your designs but not too large for your inventory to fill.

Before committing to a retail space lease, consider the following questions:

- Do you plan to use the space to sell clothing or to publicize your line?

- How much inventory will you have to sell to pay the rent?

- Will you be required to keep your store staffed and open during certain days and hours?

🖈 Will you need to hire additional staff to help operate the store?

🖈 Do you have the time to operate a retail business in addition to your fashion design business?

🖈 Do the businesses around the location support the image you are trying to create for your label?

🖈 Do you have the funds to decorate the space so it appeals to your target market?

🖈 Do you have enough pieces on hand to make the store profitable?

When scouting potential retail space, take notes about the size and shape of each location. List any furnishings or decorations you would need to purchase to make the space reflect the image of your line. Investigate both the foot traffic and the vehicle traffic that pass the location. Pay attention to how easy it is to find the location and whether there is ample room for parking.

The following worksheet, also found on the accompanying CD, can help you compare the attributes of potential retail sales sites.

RETAIL SITE COMPARISON WORKSHEET			
	Site 1	Site 2	Site 3
Address			
Contact name			
Contact telephone number			
Date visited			
Width			
Length			
Square footage			

RETAIL SITE COMPARISON WORKSHEET			
	Site 1	**Site 2**	**Site 3**
Lighting			
Furnishing			
Storage			
Entrance			
Handicap accessibility			
Signs			
Location			
Parking			
Foot traffic			
Vehicle traffic			
Appeal to target market			
Other notes			

Internet Sales

If you decide to retail your own clothing, you may choose to sell online. The Internet allows new fashion design businesses to show their lines to customers half a world away. If you decide to retail online, you can sell your garments on your own Web site, at online auction sites, through other Web sites as an affiliate, or a combination of these strategies.

Selling on your own Web site allows you complete freedom in pricing and displaying your clothes. You can design the entire site around the image you want to create for your label. However, it can be difficult for casual Web surfers to find new designers. If you create specialized or unique apparel, it will be easier to drive traffic to your site than if you produce clothes similar to those which consumers can find at their local mall.

Listing your apparel on Internet auction sites, such as eBay or Etsy, can help you sell merchandise, bring visitors to your Web site, and increase customer recognition of your brand. You do not need to carry a large inventory to sell at these sites because you can list each piece individually. Most auction sites have templates you can use to set up your listings.

Many people come to online auction Web sites looking for bargains, so you may not be able to charge full retail price for your apparel. You have to pay a listing fee, and if you do make a sale, you may have to pay part of the final value on top of that. Despite these disadvantages, online auctions can be used to clear out old merchandise or pieces with sizing or construction flaws. If you are selling seconded inventory, be sure to describe the piece thoroughly. If the piece you are selling has quality problems, consider removing your tag so that your reputation is not affected.

Some retailers may list your products on their Web sites. If you are a new company and find that you are getting few visitors to your own site, you may increase your sales by affiliating with a more established and popular site. Affiliate sales programs may limit the price you can charge for your apparel. In addition, the host site may take a percentage of the sales price.

Wholesale Options

You may decide to market your designs to retailers, who then sell them to consumers. By wholesaling your line, you give up some independence; for example, you may not get to choose how the garments are displayed in the store or how they are marketed, but you are freed from the time and money required to establish a retail operation.

To wholesale your designs to retail chains, you will need to rent showroom space at a trade show or market center and arrange for corporate buyers to review your line. Competition for large retail contracts is fierce, and buyers from department stores or chain apparel stores may be less likely to take a chance on unknown designers. However, you can learn about the wholesale process by attending a trade show or market week even if you do not land a huge order.

Local boutiques are a good place for small fashion designers to start wholesaling. Independent stores often seek to differentiate themselves from larger chains by offering unique or exclusive products and may be eager to work with a new designer. Even if the owners are not convinced your line would appeal to their customers, they might be willing to give you some insight about your target market. They may offer to host a trunk show in order to gauge customer response or to take some pieces on consignment.

When retailers take garments on consignment, they display the clothing for the designer for a time or until the clothing is sold. The designer still owns the clothing, and no money is exchanged between the retailer and the designer until a customer purchases a garment.

Once the consigned property is sold, the retailer and the designer each get a percentage of the sale price. Usually the designer receives 60 percent to 70 percent of the price and the retailer keeps the remainder.

For retailers, consignment sales are a low-risk way to add inventory to their shop, see how their customers react to different styles, and start relationships with new designers. For designers, it is a way to get more exposure and test the market for a particular style.

Many designers avoid consignment arrangements because of the financial risk. In a wholesale agreement, the designer gets paid regardless of whether the retailer can sell the apparel or not. Under the typical consignment agreement, the designer manufactures the garments and provides the retailer with inventory, but if the clothing does not sell, the designer does not recoup any money.

Once a retailer expresses interest in your designs, do not be in a rush to sign the contract. Make sure you can meet the delivery schedule and the pricing allows you to cover your expenses and make a reasonable profit.

A wholesale contract is often written to allow the buyer 30 to 90 days to pay the invoice after the buyer receives the merchandise. This puts you in the position of extending credit to your buyers, which is not a decision to take lightly. Before signing a wholesale contract, make sure that your buyers are good credit risks. One way to do this is to ask for references. You can also check the business's credit report through Dun & Bradstreet (**www.dnb.com**). Dun & Bradstreet compiles information about companies' payment histories, annual sales, bankruptcies, liens, and legal judgments. For a fee, you can access the information and use it to evaluate if you should extend credit to a buyer.

The standard terms of a wholesale contract may leave you with too little cash on hand to fill additional orders or to create samples for next season's line. Some financial institutions are willing to extend credit using accounts receivable as collateral. Another option is "factoring" or "accounts receivable financing," where you sell outstanding invoices in exchange for cash.

Factoring usually puts money in your account quicker than applying for a loan would. Factors, the companies that buy invoices, often have lower credit requirements than lenders. Another advantage of factoring is you do not have to worry about collecting accounts. That becomes the factor's responsibility.

Factoring can be more expensive than a traditional business loan. The factor usually takes a set percentage of the invoice value, and there may be other associated fees. Accounts receivable financing is not as highly regulated as the lending industry, but it puts working capital into your hands quickly.

The following chart, also found on the accompanying CD, can help you compare offers from different buyers.

WHOLESALE OFFER COMPARISON WORKSHEET	Offer 1	Offer 2	Offer 3	Offer 4
Business name				
Business telephone				
Business address				
Contact name				
Contact telephone				
Collection viewed				
Date collection viewed				
Location of collection viewing				
Order date				
Style ordered				
Sizes ordered				
Unit price				
Subtotal				
Style ordered				
Sizes ordered				
Unit price				
Subtotal				
Style ordered				
Sizes ordered unit price subtotal				
ORDER TOTAL				
Delivery date				
Payment terms				
Exclusivity terms				
Date contract signed				

Pricing Your Product

Whether you sell directly to the consumer or to retail businesses, you should price your pieces before potential customers see them. Otherwise, you risk looking unprepared and unprofessional or undercharging for your work.

When pricing your clothes, consider the cost of materials, the amount of time involved in designing, the price of making the patterns and samples, and the manufacturing expenses for each individual piece.

A common pricing strategy is to multiply the material and manufacturing costs of each style by 2.2 to 2.8. When you consider the money you pay for rent, utility, licenses, and consultants to keep your business running, this should yield about 15 percent in profit. If the profit is lower than 15 percent, consider ways to lower the cost of creating the apparel.

Retail prices are often calculated by multiplying the wholesale price by 2.2 to 2.8. This helps retailers cover their operating expenses and clear a profit.

Before you set prices for the apparel in your line, research the prices of comparable items. If your prices are going to be much higher or lower, be prepared to tell the customer why. For example, your shirts may be more expensive than a similar shirt at a local department store because they are made out of an expensive fabric or individually fitted to the wearer. Do not be afraid to charge more for higher quality, but be prepared to justify the price.

You may find that there is a piece in your collection that has a particularly high production cost because of the detailing or materials used. Once the wholesale and retail markups have been added, this piece may be priced out of the range of your target market. One way to equalize prices within your collection is price averaging.

Price averaging is the practice of averaging the costs of two different styles. This lowers the price of an expensive garment and raises the cost of a design that is cheaper to produce.

For example, consider a leather jacket that costs $100 per unit to manufacture and a blouse that costs $4. After standard wholesale and retail markups, the jacket would end up costing the consumer $484 to $784. The blouse would be priced between about $20 and $30.

After researching the target market and comparable lines, the designer may decide that not many jackets will be sold at $500. If the production costs of the shirt are averaged with those of the jacket and it is assumed that ten blouses will be sold per jacket, the jacket can be wholesaled at $154 to $196 (retail price $338-$548) and the blouse for $22 to $28 (retail price $48 to $78).

Another common pricing strategy is target costing. In target costing, you choose materials and styles that will allow you to meet specific retail price points. The price points are based on the maximum amount you expect a customer to pay for a type of garment.

For example, a designer's research may indicate that a typical customer in the target market is willing to pay up to $75 for a pair of jeans. This means the price to the wholesaler would be between $26 and $34. The manufacturing material costs to produce each pair of jeans would have to be between $9 and $15 to allow for 220 percent to 280 percent markup. The designer would then choose the fabric, fasteners, style, and details that would allow for hitting that targeted price.

The following worksheet, also found on the accompanying CD, summarizes this basic pricing equation.

GARMENT PRICING WORKSHEET	
Number of garments manufactured:	A
Total cost of materials:	B
Total cost of manufacturing:	C
B + C = total cost:	D
D/A = cost per garment:	E
E x 2.2 = minimum wholesale price per garment:	F
E x 2.8 = maximum wholesale price per garment:	G

GARMENT PRICING WORKSHEET	
F x 2.2 = minimum retail price per garment:	H.
G x 2.8 = maximum retail price per garment:	I.

CASE STUDY: CASTLE GARDEN CREATIONS

Karen Farris, Co-owner
Castle Garden Creations
www.castlegardencreations.com
7205 Bayless Lane
Powell, TN 37849
865-947-8900

My twin sister, Karla Hood, and I started Castle Garden Creations because we both have a love of sewing and history. I had been in the sewing business for about 25 years, and she studied theatrical costuming in college. We put our heads together and decided to jump in. We started small by buying fabric retail and working out of our homes.

Karla and I are very close. We think alike and sometimes have disagreements, but working together gives us a great support system. We are active in a historical reenactment organization and sell our clothes at two of their largest events.

We believe that everything works together to create the entire effect. If you want to feel like you have stepped back into another era, you have to think about all your surroundings. To help our customers do this, we have developed our Web site into a "one stop shop" with gifts, tapestries, and historical recipes.

My advice for new business owners is to start small. Do your research and find a niche doing what you know and love.

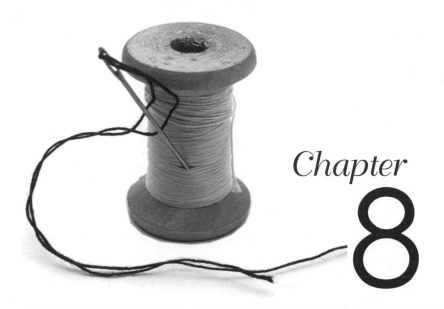

Chapter 8

Manufacturing

W hether you plan to retail your apparel yourself or sell it through department stores, you will need garments to fulfill your purchase orders. If you plan on making small or single runs of your designs, you are a skilled sewer, and you have professional-grade equipment, you may be able to manufacture the clothing yourself. As your orders grow larger, however, you may decide to contract out the manufacturing so you can devote more time to designing subsequent lines.

Suppliers

Whether you construct your own garments or use a factory, you need to purchase all the material, fasteners, and trim used in your designs. You can find potential suppliers by visiting trade shows, textile mills, and fabric warehouses. You can also research online fabric wholesalers. To find recommendations, ask the contractor or factory that sewed your samples. Talk to other designers about where they like to buy fabric.

Before visiting a mill or warehouse, check to see if you need to set up an appointment with a sales representative. When you meet with the representative, make sure you are prepared. Know what you want so that you do not waste time. Think about possible substitutions in case the supplier does not have exactly what you want, but do not change your entire design.

If possible, visit several potential suppliers. Discuss purchase minimums, payment terms, return policy, and delivery times. Make a note of how long they will carry the material you are interested in using in case a buyer increases a purchase order. Find out where the material comes from and the supplier's policy on purchasing from factories that use underage, underpaid, or illegal workers.

Ask for a sample of all the materials you use or order a little extra so that you can test the care instructions and make sure they are appropriate.

If you purchase materials in person, be sure to look for color and weave flaws before you leave the supplier. Bring along a tape measure and check to make sure the labeled fabric width is correct. Watch while the lengths of fabric are measured, and ask any questions before the fabric is cut.

If you have your purchase delivered to your studio or manufacturer, check the order thoroughly before any garments are made. Check all measurements. Look for flaws in the fabric. Compare what you ordered with what you received.

Manufacturers

Choose your manufacturer with the same care you designed your line.

Before signing a contract, check out as many alternatives as you can. Ask for recommendations from your suppliers and other designers. Call local trade unions and organizations. If possible, visit the factories and look at the working conditions. Look at garments the factory has produced to make sure they meet your quality requirements.

Some manufacturers may have minimum production runs. If your order does not meet the minimum, discuss any options available. Can items that have similar cutting or construction requirements be grouped together to meet the minimum? If you are willing to wait longer for your order, will they lower the minimum?

Get a quote from every manufacturer you consider, but the cheapest manufacturing option is not always the best deal. Research the factory's other clients. Does the manufacturer have experience making clothes like yours? What is its reputation in the industry?

Make sure that the manufacturer you choose has the necessary business licenses and insurance coverage. Does it use illegal workers or business practices? If the factory you use becomes the center of an employment scandal, your company's image could be tarnished.

Discuss penalties for late deliveries and coverage of damaged goods. Make sure you are satisfied with the way the manufacturing services contract addresses these issues.

What If You Are Not Satisfied?

If you are not satisfied with a shipment from a supplier or manufacturer, contact the company's sales representative immediately. Stay calm and professional and try to negotiate a replacement or refund. If you cannot come to an agreement, you may want to contact an attorney. Fashion is a tight industry. If you are too much of a pest over small details, you may find that other contractors will not work with you.

If you find a supplier or manufacturer who offers you a better deal, think carefully before alienating your current associates. You may need them if you have an unexpected rush order that the new company cannot accommodate or if the better deal turns sour.

Packaging Your Pieces

Whether you sell to retailers or directly to the consumer, you will need to get your garments from your workshop or warehouse to your customer.

If you are selling to a retail establishment, it probably has established packing and shipping protocols. Make sure to read the directions carefully. If you ignore the procedures, you risk damaging your working relationship and having your shipments refused.

If the company you are shipping to did not give you detailed instructions, do not be afraid to ask for clarification. A shipping agreement may include:

- The mailing address where you should ship the clothing

- Routing numbers for different types of garments

- The company's preferred shipping method

- A list of required documentation that should accompany your shipment

- Packaging requirements listing what garments should be folded, hung, or wrapped

✣ Labeling specifications for the clothing

✣ The preferred labeling format for the shipping boxes

If you are shipping your clothing directly to your customers, you have more freedom in how you package your garments. Your shipping and packing choices reflect your image and should appeal to your target market. If you sell high-priced fashions, your customers may expect glossy boxes holding tissue-wrapped products that have been pressed and are ready to wear. If you sell clothes made from organic fibers to environmentally conscious customers, recycled packing materials may be more appropriate.

Although it is not always possible to pack garments so they are ready to wear, take the time to make sure your clothes arrive in the best possible shape. Folding with tissue paper can help soften creases and reduce wrinkling. Cardboard can be used to shape garments and keep them looking crisp. Make your customers glad they ordered your designs, not disappointed. Consider enclosing a catalog or other marketing material that fits with the image you are trying to create for your business.

In either a retail or wholesale situation, provide a packing slip to help your customers compare what they ordered with what they received. Consider insuring large, fragile, expensive, or irreplaceable orders. Delivery tracking services help you find missing shipments and help your customers know when to expect their packages.

Labeling

The Federal Trade Commission sets the standards for labeling apparel and household fashions. Most of the requirements are spelled out in the Textile and Wool Acts and the Care Labeling Rule. The purpose of these regulations is to make sure customers know what they are purchasing.

The Textile and Wool Acts

Most textiles and wool products must be labeled with three key pieces of information:

- Fiber content

- Country or countries of origin

- Product manufacturer

These labels must be applied before the finished product is sold to the customer. If the product is in an intermediate stage, the information can be included on the invoice instead of on a label. The invoice must also include the name and address of the issuing person or company. However, if the product is substantially finished, it needs to be labeled. A coat that needs only the buttons added or a skirt that only needs to be hemmed, for example, are considered substantially finished and should be labeled in compliance with the Textile and Wool Acts.

Manufacturers can put the required information on a single label or use different labels to disclose fiber content, country of origin, and product manufacturer. Whichever method you choose, the labels must be easy to find and read. You can add some information beyond what is required; however, you may not include anything inaccurate, deceptive, or misleading.

All disclosures must appear in English, but you may include additional languages if you wish. Except for some country names, abbreviations are not allowed in the required disclosures. Labels do not have to be sewn into the garments, but they must be attached so they remain securely affixed until the clothes reach the final consumer. If you are importing goods, customs may require that certain labels be sewn to the garments.

You are required to keep records of the labels you placed on your garments on file for at least three years.

Fiber Content

If a product is covered by the Textile or Wool Acts, the label must show the generic name for all fibers used. In addition, the percentage by weight for each fiber must be listed. The fiber with the highest percentage by weight must be listed first, followed by the other component fibers in descending order. If only one fiber is used in the garment, the label may say "All" instead of "100%." For example, a suit made only of silk may be labeled "All Silk" or "Silk 100%." All fiber components must be listed using equal weighted and sized letters. The components must appear close to each other on the label.

In most cases, only fibers used in quantities greater than or equal to 5 percent by weight are listed. Instead, small components can be counted together and listed as "other fibers" at the bottom of the fiber content list. The main exception to this rule is wool, which must be listed when used in any amount. If other fibers are used for a definite function, you may disclose the amount used if you like. For example, if a fabric includes 3 percent spandex for elasticity, you can list that amount on the label.

Different rules apply for trim, decorations, pile fabrics, specialty wool fibers, and trademarked fibers that may be parts of your garments. Trim such as collars, findings, bindings, and gussets are not included in label requirements. Decorations that cover 15 percent or less of the garment's surface area, threads used to sew the apparel, and linings not used to add warmth are also excluded. However, decorative trim that covers more than 15 percent of the item's surface and is made of a fiber different than the base fabric must be labeled. In addition, if you referenced the fiber used in the decoration in another label, description, or advertisement, you must label the decoration's contents even if it covers less than 15 percent of the garment's surface area. For example, if you describe a jacket as having "silk detailing" because of a small amount of silk embroidery on one pocket, the label may read, "Body: 100% Nylon. Decoration: 100% Silk." If you did not mention the decoration in the description, the label could read "100% nylon exclusive of decoration."

Ornamentation refers to fibers used to create a pattern or design in fabric. Fibers used in fabric ornamentation must be disclosed if they compose more than 5 percent of the product's total fiber weight. Because it can be difficult to differentiate between trim and ornamentation, decorative patterns or designs must be labeled for fiber content if the decoration covers more than 15 percent of the surface area and accounts for more than 5 percent of the garment's fiber weight. If either of those cases is not true, then the label does not have to include the fiber contents of the design. Instead, the label can read, "exclusive of decoration" or, "exclusive of ornamentation" after the fiber list for the body of the garment.

Linings, fillings, and pads do not have to be included in fiber content lists as long as they are used only for structural purposes. If the component is used for warmth, if you refer to the contents of the component in a description or advertisement, or if the component includes wool, the fiber contents must be disclosed. In that case, the label should differentiate between the body of the garment and the lining, filling, or padding. For example, the label for a winter coat might read, "Shell: 100% Leather. Lining: 100% Nylon. Filling: 80% Wool, 20% Cotton." Even if the lining is made of the same fabric as the body of the garment, it should be separated in the label. For example, a jacket might be labeled, "Shell: 100% Nylon. Lining: 100% Nylon."

Likewise, if different parts of a piece are made out of different fibers, the label should disclose this. For example, the label for a wedding dress might read, "Bodice: 100% Silk. Skirt: 85% Nylon, 15% Silk."

Country of Origin

All garments and textiles must be labeled to disclose where they were processed or manufactured. You can use the phrase, "Made in the U.S.A." only if every step of your manufacturing process occurs in the United States and you use only materials that are also from the United States.

If you use products from another country, your label must say where each component came from. The label must also say what assembly processes occurred in what countries. A label on a dress, for instance, might read, "Assembled in Mexico. Hemmed in the U.S.A."

The country of origin label should not be covered by another label. For garments with necks, such as shirts, coats, and jackets, the country of origin label needs to be attached at or near the inside center of the neck. For other types of clothing and textiles, the label must be in an obvious and easy-to-read location.

Manufacturer Identification

The third type of required information for most garment and textile labels is the name or Registered Identification Number (RN) of the manufacturer.

If you choose to use a company name, it must be the name as it appears on your business documents, such as contracts, invoices, and bills. Alternatively, you can apply for an RN through the Federal Trade Commission at **FTC.gov.**

Special Labeling Rules for Furs

In addition to identifying fiber content, country or countries of origin, and manufacturer, garments made with animal fur have special labeling requirements.

If you are producing fashions that use fur, you must label the garment with the name of the animal. If the fur is imported, you must list the country of origin. The FTC requires that you indicate if the fur is natural or if it has been chemically treated, such as dyed or bleached. If the fur is used or damaged, or if more than 10 percent of the garment's surface area is made of pieces, including waste fur, ears, or tails, this must be revealed in the labeling.

The Care Labeling Rule

The Federal Trade Commission also sets rules about how manufacturers communicate care instructions to potential customers. These rules help consumers pick clothing with care requirements that fit their life styles.

Textile wearing apparel or piece goods that are used to make wearing apparel are required to have permanent labels with clear care instructions. Shoes, gloves, hats, handkerchiefs, belts, suspenders, and disposable items are exempt.

Before you sell any garment you manufacture, you must determine complete instructions for regular care. It is your responsibility to make sure that these instructions will not substantially harm the garment. If the item cannot be cleaned without harm, you must disclose this to the buyer. Customers also need to be informed about any reasonable procedures that may injure the clothing. For example, some garments should not be ironed, heat dried, or machine washed. These warnings, along with the care instructions, must be on an easy-to-find label that will remain attached and readable for the life of the garment.

You must have a reasonable basis for any care instructions you give. Labeling every garment, "Dry Clean Only" is not in the spirit of the FTC Care Label Rule. The care instructions you provide can be based on your experience and industry expertise or by testing the materials used to manufacture the clothing. Even if you test all the fabric separately, you are still required to have "reasonable evidence" that your care instructions will not damage the completed garment. This means you must be careful that your instructions will not cause part of the item to shrink or bleed.

Care labels must be attached to your garments before they are sold. The labels are required to be easy to find and permanent. The care instructions, although not necessarily the care label, must be visible when the garment is displayed for sale. If all the pieces sold together as a set have the same care instructions, then only one piece needs to have a care label. However, if the pieces are sold separately or if one or more components have different care instructions, all the pieces need to have care labels.

There are some exceptions to the care label rule. Reversible garments that do not have pockets can have temporary labels. These labels still need to be placed so that the customer has no trouble finding them. In addition, clothing that can be bleached, dried, dry cleaned, washed, or ironed using the harshest procedures can have a temporary label that says, "Wash or dry clean, any normal method."

Other products may be granted exemptions by the FTC. Be sure to complete an exemption application and wait for approval before selling your items without care labels, as you may be charged up to $11,000 for each noncompliance offense.

Contacting the FTC

For more information about labeling requirements, to receive a Registered Identification Number, or to apply for an exemption to a labeling rule, contact the Federal Trade Commission:

Federal Trade Commission
www.ftc.gov
1-877-FTC-HELP (1-877-382-4357)

FTC Consumer Response Center
600 Pennsylvania Avenue NW
Washington, D.C. 20580

CASE STUDY: JIM'S FORMAL WEAR COMPANY

Steven Davis, Vice President of Marketing
Jim's Formal Wear Company
www.jimsfw.com
One Tuxedo Park
PO Box 125
Trenton, IL 62293
618-224-9211

Quality merchandise and service at a fair price were the foundation on which Jim Davis built his business. He was the owner and operator of Jim's Men's and Boys' Store, a successful men's apparel shop established by his father. The store was located in the small town of Trenton, Illinois, 35 miles from downtown St. Louis, Missouri. Jim's outstanding reputation in this rural community was based on his commitment to serve his customers with the finest merchandise available.

Jim offered tuxedos for rental through a wholesale formalwear supplier in nearby St. Louis. Unfortunately, the quality and service he received from this company did not meet his expectations. More important, it did not meet the expectations of his customers. On one occasion, a longtime customer was so dissatisfied with the quality of a tuxedo that he quit shopping at Jim's Men's and Boys' Store for any of his clothing needs. These situations were frustrating to Jim. His store's reputation, something for which he had worked long and hard to build up, was suffering. Finally, he decided to do something about it.

Prior to owning his own men's store, Jim traveled Southern Illinois and Missouri as a manufacturer's representative. His character, honesty, and salesmanship earned him many friends in the men's wear business. He called these old friends and soon learned that they, too, were frustrated with their formalwear supplier. Jim asked their support if he would provide quality tuxedos and service at a fair price. Everyone said they would back him in his new venture.

CASE STUDY: JIM'S FORMAL WEAR COMPANY

Jim's Formal Wear was born in 1964 when Jim purchased 200 black coats, 200 white coats, and 50 dozen formal shirts. He started his fledgling business in a small 900-square foot house near the men's store and had no idea what the next 40 years would bring.

In 1984, misfortune struck as Jim suffered a heart attack and underwent major surgery. The doctors told him it was time to give up his successful formalwear business. Fortunately, Jim and his wife, Betty, had two sons who had grown up with the business. Gary and Mike were actively involved and controlled various aspects of the rapidly growing company.

In September of that year, the youngest son, Gary, purchased the company from his father and brother. Mike then moved to California where he opened up his own very successful retail tuxedo shop. Jim passed away in February 1996.

Under Gary's leadership, the company began focusing its efforts solely on wholesale distribution. Today, Jim's Formal Wear Company is known as "the largest wholesale formalwear rental company in the world." Its 10 strategically located facilities total more than 300,000 square feet of office, production, and warehouse space. It is true that the operation of 10 facilities is more costly, but this allows Jim's to service its customers to be thorough and effective. Jim Davis' founding principle of "Quality Merchandise & Service at a Fair Price" has remained company's philosophy.

Our wholesale business is fairly unusual in that we are a rental company. We will typically decide on what new styles to purchase only one time every year (August). This purchase will usually include about four new styles. These styles will remain in our merchandise assortment for approximately five years.

Prior to purchasing from a company, they must agree to the following:

1.) JFW takes pride in providing the highest-quality garments in the industry. All garments must be tested prior to presenting them to us. Manufacturers we purchase from understand how to produce a garment that can be worn and dry cleaned more than 25 times.

   They must be able to prove their garments can withstand 25 dry cleanings before we will consider the garment. Some manufacturers will have their

CASE STUDY: JIM'S FORMAL WEAR COMPANY

products tested by the International Fabricare Institute to provide further proof of the quality of their construction.

2.) JFW takes pride in the level of service and on-time delivery we provide our customers. Our business is seasonal. It is important that we take delivery of new garments by the middle of February to be sure we are able to deliver to our customers on time. Hard orders will be placed by the middle of October. A manufacturer's inability to deliver on time would sour a relationship with our company.

3.) We believe our manufacturers should share the risk in the purchase of new styles. We require a minimum of a 50 percent nonobligatory reserve be stocked ready for delivery over and above the quantity of merchandise ordered. This merchandise would be released for sale to the general public sometime in April if it is not needed. Manufacturers that are willing to stock more than a 50 percent reserve will be placed as the first entry in our contact list.

4.) Manufacturers must be quick to respond to any issues we face in terms of quality or delivery.

5.) Manufacturers must be willing to provide terms. More favorable terms will make that manufacturer first on our contact list.

6.) All products must be priced comparable to competitive products in the marketplace.

Ability to meet or exceed these requirements will make conditions favorable to do business with a particular manufacturer. Inability to meet these conditions would quickly sour a relationship with our company. We take great pride in being an easy supplier for our customers to do business with. Our quality and on-time delivery standards are unparalleled in our industry. We expect nothing less from our suppliers. We are only as good as the people we buy from.

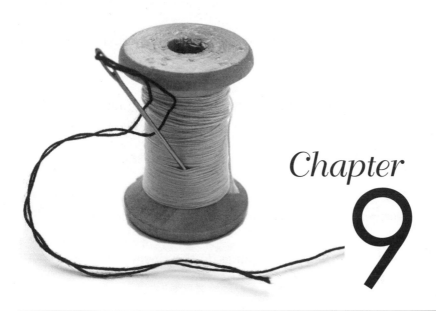

Marketing

Marketing is the art of convincing customers to choose your designs over competitors'. If you plan to sell your line to retailers, you will need to convince the boutique owners or store buyers that your styles will appeal to their shoppers. If you sell directly to the consumer, you need to convince them that your apparel is the best value available.

Understanding Your Market

Without customers, your fashion design business cannot be profitable. Understanding your target market is one of the first and most important steps toward successfully marketing your line.

When researching your market, try to answer the following questions:

- What makes your potential customers different than the general population?

- Does your target market have any specialized clothing needs? Winter athletes, for example, need lightweight performance gear that can be worn in layers.

- Do your customers have any life style needs? For instance, vegans need garments that are not made of animal products.

- Besides clothing, what other things do they spend money on?

- Where do your customers live?

- Where do members of your target market tend to shop?

- What is the average age and income of your customers?

- As a group, will they be reaching any lifespan milestones soon?

For example, women in their late 20s may be planning for children. Teens may be preparing to go to college.

Look at the position of your market now and think about possible future trends. A starting point for research is the U.S. Census Bureau (**www.census. gov**), where you can find population demographic data. Next, contact magazines, newspapers, and Web sites geared toward your target market. Choose periodicals that would be good places to advertise your line. Ask for their media kit, which should include their current advertisement rates in addition to information about how their readers spend their money.

The more you know about your customers, the better you will be able to create a profitable image and brand for your company.

Image

Your company's image is how customers see you. Most businesses want their target market to view them as a better value than the competition. This does not necessarily mean being the cheapest. If you wholesale your apparel to large department stores, you might want the buyers to see your company as one that always meets deadlines and fixes problems quickly and fairly. Even if your clothes are more expensive than another designer, buyers might see yours as a better value because of your reliability.

Whether an image is good or bad depends on the viewer. For example, consider a designer who sells trendy party clothes. Although the clothes are not made out of high-quality material, to teenagers who want to have the edgiest outfits, the styles are a good value. To their parents, shirts that will be torn or out of style within a few weeks are a waste of money. If the designer is marketing his products to teenagers, the image is appropriate.

Every business has an image. In the fashion industry, your image is influenced by a combination of elements, including the designs you produce, the stores that carry your line, the advertisements you run, reviews your designs receive, the type of people who wear your products, the quality of your apparel, the customer service you provide, your logo, and the cost of your merchandise.

If your target market does not see your designs as a good value, you may find your profits slowing because fewer people buy your clothes. To change your company's image, look at the unit prices of more popular labels and compare them to yours. Address any quality control or customer service issues. Examine the stores that carry your clothing and determine if they portray the image you want to create for your label. Consider using advertisements or public relations events to help change how your target market sees you.

Branding

Companies often use images and words to help consumers differentiate between their products and the competitors'. This is called branding. In fashion design, the goal of branding is often to have customers recognize and prefer your designs.

Branding your apparel is easier if your designs are easy to identify. You can accomplish this by using a signature image, cut, or design element throughout your collection. For example, if most of your shirts and skirts have bright blue hem tape, customers will learn to associate that detail with your label.

Branding works hand in hand with image. The best situation is if customers recognize your designs through effective branding and prefer them, or even better, insist on them, because of the appealing image.

To develop a brand, first list the attributes of your designs. Attributes are simply the facts about your apparel's construction and style. For example, all your clothing may be manufactured of natural, domestically grown, organic cotton. Next, consider your target market's values. Use these values to turn the attributes into benefits. If your target market is soccer moms, they may appreciate the easy care of cotton and the lack of potentially irritating dyes. Baby boomers might be swayed by the patriotism of using domestic fibers. Environmentally conscious young adults may respond to the use of a renewable resource grown without pesticides.

After you have identified the benefits to your target market, select a name, logo, or slogan that encapsulates that benefit. If you are stressing the easy care of the fabric, perhaps use a slogan such as, "less time in the laundry room, more time for fun." An eagle or variation of the flag could remind customers about the domestically grown material. A stylized river or globe sums up the environmental benefits of the line.

Strengthening Your Image and Brand

Many business decisions have an effect on your label's image and branding. If you decide to use a licensed image or slogan, make sure your choice supports how you want people to see your company. If you want to appeal to conservative baby boomers, a line of shirts featuring pictures of Che Guevara may not be the best choice to improve your image.

Place your clothing in stores that also support the benefits your target market wants. If your customers want the most contemporary European-inspired styles, they may skip a designer whose clothing is carried at the same store where they buy their light bulbs.

To build a strong brand, make sure your future designs incorporate the same benefits customers associate with your label. Once consumers begin to recognize your signature hardware on high-quality leatherwear, for example, if you begin to put the same hardware on cheap synthetics, you may devalue the brand.

If you are having trouble branding or molding your image into the one you want, consider hiring a marketing consultant. Someone without a personal connection to your business may be better positioned to pinpoint inconsistencies in your products or performance and the way you want to be seen by your customers. A good marketing professional can help you create a strategy to correct these problems. If you choose to use a marketing consultant, look for one with experience in the fashion industry. Ask for references and check with previous clients to make sure they were satisfied with the advice they received.

Developing Your Logo

A logo can be a powerful branding tool. You can use your logo on apparel hangtags and labels; on the clothing itself in the form of prints, appliqués, or hardware; on your company Web site; in public relations events; and on marketing and advertising material. A well-designed logo reinforces your image and helps customers recognize your company.

Logo design software is an easy and inexpensive way to create a logo for your company. Most programs have templates and libraries of images to help amateurs make nice-looking logos. The finished product can be saved in a variety of digital formats.

If you create your own logo, be sure your design looks good in both color and black and white so you can use it in a variety of graphical settings.

Stock templates and images often yield generic-looking logos. A professional graphic artist can help you develop a logo that better fits your business and supports your brand. Although hiring a consultant may be more expensive than buying a software pack, a qualified graphic artist will know how different fonts and graphics can be combined to create a certain image and help you develop ad layouts that will work well with your logo.

Online Marketing

A professional Web site is a valuable marketing asset for a new fashion design company. Through your Web site, you can communicate with potential customers and show off your latest styles. Even if you are on a tight budget and working out of your bedroom, your Web site can give your business an image of glamour and sophistication. Although your printing budget may limit the number of pages in your catalog, on your Web site you can put multiple views of each garment and update them as often as you want.

Online marketing extends beyond creating a company Web site. There are many inexpensive or free ways to use the Internet to promote your business. Visit message boards and join discussion groups that are popular with your target market. Not only is this a good opportunity to research your customer base, but if you participate in the conversations, you may find ways to mention your designs or link to your Web site. Avoid blatant commercial posts, but do not be afraid to talk about your business as part of a larger online conversation. Unless a forum's rules prohibit it, include your Web site in your signature so that it appears at the end of all your posts.

In addition to developing a business Web site, consider establishing a presence at a social networking site such as Facebook or MySpace. Social networking sites allow you to connect with other people based on common interests, acquaintances, experiences, or geographic location. For certain target markets, this networking can be an efficient way of creating buzz and interest about your line.

E-mail is another inexpensive way to reach a large number of potential customers. Be sure to send marketing e-mails only to people who have opted into your mailing list during a purchase or through your Web site. Unsolicited commercial e-mail, or spam, may irritate the recipients and violate your ISP user agreement. Sending spam is illegal in some areas.

Direct Marketing

Direct marketing is sending information about your products to potential customers by mail. Direct mailings can range from simple postcards featuring one picture of a garment in your collection to complete catalogs with multiple views of every style you have available for purchase.

Look Books

If you plan on selling your fashions wholesale, a "look book" is an important direct marketing tool that you can send to boutique owners and buyers for chain stores. You should produce a look book each season to showcase your current collection. Include at least one good picture of each garment in your line. You may decide to include more than one so you can use artistic images along with those that focus on the clothing.

Your look book needs to support the image of your company. If your image is earthy and laid-back, photographs with urban or formal settings may not work as well as a more natural background would. Your look book is a chance to show your line creatively, so there are no hard rules about layouts or binding. It is a good idea to include an identification number and description of each piece, as well as your contact information, to make it easy for a customer to make a purchase.

You can produce a look book as cheaply or expensively as you wish. On the frugal end of the spectrum, you can take pictures of your clothes on volunteer models, develop full-size prints at a print store and slide them into an attractive folder with a mounted business card. If you have a larger marketing budget, you may decide to use a professional photographer, established models, and a graphic designer to help put together a glossy publication.

The photographs you use in your look book should show the movement, detail, and drape of each design. This may require a photographer with experience shooting fashion. When choosing a photographer, be sure to review his or her portfolio and follow up on references.

There are some ways to display garments without using a model, but the right body wearing your clothes can show off the line and movement of your design and help support your company's image. For your look book, you can use the same model for every outfit to help cut costs and create unity throughout the publication.

Think about your target market when selecting a model. Have a look in mind before you contact a modeling agency. Choose someone whose look embodies the ideals your customers want for themselves. If you design evening wear, select someone sleek and classy. If you design athletic clothing, use a model who looks fit and strong.

Professional hairstyle and makeup artists can help create a look that will highlight particular features in your designs or create a mood. If you decide not to use a professional, work with the model before the shoot to come up with an appealing style.

The background and props you use for the photo shoot can help develop the tone of the look book, enhance the image of your line, show the inspiration behind the collection, and define your target market. Dressing the shots is important, but too many props or a complex background can take the viewers' focus off of the clothes. If you have trouble creating a compelling but not overwhelming scene to showcase your designs, consider hiring a professional set stylist.

Brochures and Postcards

You can use the photographs from your look book to make brochures and postcards to introduce potential customers to your line. These can be sent to company buyers to invite them to look at your collection during a trade event, or they can be sent directly to consumers to entice them to look at your Web site or attend a trunk show.

Catalogs

A catalog can encourage old customers to place new orders and let potential new customers see your line. Make your catalog something that recipients want to keep and read for a while by using attractive photographs, descriptions of your garments, and added-value inserts such as fashion articles and tips. The more often someone looks at your catalog, the more likely he or she is to find something to purchase.

Press Kits

Press kits are marketing tools that you send directly to editors in hopes they will review or mention your line. A good press kit should include your look book, a designer biography, clips of previous reviews, and a summary of the collection. The collection summary should mention the inspiration behind the collection, your target market, and stores that carry the line. You can package your press kit in a two-pocket folder.

Sales Kits

Sales kits are sent to buyers and boutique owners who you hope will carry your line. Like a press kit, a sales kit can be contained in a two-pocket folder. In addition to a look book, biography, and collection summary, include line sheets for your current collection. Line sheets are technical specifications and line drawings of each garment. If you design accessories, simple photographs of each piece in front of a plain, contrasting background may be substituted for drawings. Your line sheets should include a detailed description and the current wholesale price for each piece. Save the flowery imagery for your catalogs and look books. Line sheets should focus on the facts of your designs.

Make it easy for buyers to place orders. Print your contact information on each section of your sales kit.

Low Cost Internal Marketing Ideas

You may be your business's best marketing tool. Go to where your target market is. Talk to potential customers about what they are looking for in clothing and customer service. Wear your own designs, and mention your company when you get compliments. Bring brochures, business cards, and catalogs with you. Ask the managers of coffee shops, book stores, beauty salons, day spas, toy stores — or anywhere else your market frequents — if you can leave marketing materials.

Try to get your designs worn wherever there may be press, including charity events or entertainment premieres. Consider loaning out samples to people who start fashion trends, but do not give out more pieces than you can afford to lose, as your garments may return to you damaged or end up mysteriously missing.

Calculating Return on Investment

The return on investment (ROI) of a marketing project lets you see how effective certain strategies are. This lets you concentrate your money and time on campaigns that are more likely to bring in sales.

The following equation is used to calculate ROI:

$$ROI = [(sales-cost)/cost] * 100$$

In this equation, "sales" is the dollar amount of sales that were directly or indirectly the result of a particular marketing effort. "Cost" is the amount of money the effort required. Marketing costs may include printing, hiring consultants and contractors, postage, and mailing lists.

It can be difficult to be certain what sales were triggered by particular marketing tools. One way is to include a promotional code for discount pricing on a brochure, catalog, or postcard. If you primarily sell over the Internet, you can use several Web addresses and print different ones on various marketing tools, then track how many visitors come to each address and how many of those visits convert to sales. The simplest, most low-tech way is to ask customers how they found out about your business.

By analyzing your monthly, quarterly, and annual returns on investments, you can decide which marketing strategies are working, what needs tweaking, and what may be costing more money than it is bringing in.

CASE STUDY: THE RUNNING SKIRT

Shannon Farley, Owner
The Running Skirt: Anatomic Global Inc.
1241 Old Temescal Road
Corona, CA 92881
1-888-739-6955
Toll-free, Monday through Friday 8 a.m. to 5 p.m. PST
www.therunningskirt.com
contact@therunningskirt.com

I founded The Running Skirt because I was frustrated with having nowhere to put my keys, MP3 player, water bottle, and identification when I ran. I have been a graphics designer for almost ten years, and I love arts and crafts so if I see something I want, I would rather get the materials and make it than buy it.

I started off by making 10 running skirts. There was a huge response, and all of a sudden I had sold 60. I decided I needed to get some professionally made. Standardizing the design and finding the right manufacturer took about a year.

What started off as a hobby became a second job, but it really is a passion. I like that my business has a fitness aspect. I have struggled with weight loss and motivation, but my business keeps me on track. I also like that I have the ability to give back to the community. One way I market my product to the running community is by participating in charity races.

The company is really just me, although my father handles the shipping logistics. Working together has been a wonderful experience. My father is an entrepreneur too, and we are able to get each other through rough patches.

I think my designs help encourage people to exercise. My skirts add a feminine touch to your workout clothes, no matter what size.

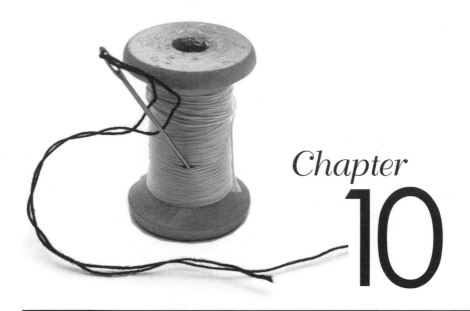

Chapter
10

Advertising & Publicity

You do not need to purchase advertisements to get your business name in the local or national press. Journalists are always looking for stories, and a newsworthy event teamed with a good press release can result in free publicity, more brand recognition, and increased sales.

Public Relations and Special Events

Special events can be effective ways of reaching new customers and receiving media coverage. Newspaper style sections often feature reviews of fashion shows. The life style page may list upcoming classes, speakers, or workshops that interest readers. Business sections may report on charitable functions of local companies.

There are many ways fashion design businesses can reach out to their communities.

Fashion Shows

You do not have to design couture garments or live in a major city to have a fashion show. A fashion show can be held as part of a trade show, in conjunction with a trunk show, or as a standalone event. Shows give buyers or consumers a chance to see your line and you the opportunity to gauge market response to new designs.

Staging a fashion show can be expensive, but depending on your budget, image, and target audience, there are many ways to cut costs.

Scheduling

After you decide to hold a fashion show, you should find a location and schedule a date. If your show will be part of a larger event, this decision may be made for you. If not, list places that members of your target market frequent. Think about which of these are large enough to set up a runway and an audience section. You will also need a convenient place for the models to change. Cross off any locations that do not fit with the image you want to create for your company. Make sure that any outdoor venues have shelter for your models and your audience in case of rain. Locations to look at include malls, parks, convention halls, recreation centers, and fairgrounds.

To save money on a location, consider teaming up with another business or with a nonprofit organization. Even businesses that are not involved in the fashion industry may be able to provide a free venue in exchange for publicity.

When scheduling your fashion show, look for dates and times that are convenient for your potential buyers. Avoid conflicts with other events that are targeted at your market. Consider repeating the fashion show throughout the day to reach more customers.

Finding and Fitting Models

One of the draws of a fashion show is seeing clothing on people. Buyers get to see how the line and fabric of a design work together.

For your fashion show, you can use professional or volunteer models. If your show is part of a charity event, the nonprofit organization may want to use donors or staff members as models. If you need additional volunteers, check with local performing art schools and agencies for models who may be willing to work in exchange for modeling credits.

Before you talk to a modeling agency, whether to ask for volunteer or professional models, decide on the look you want. Do you want your models to look sexy, athletic, or innocent? Is your image more punk rock or soccer mom? Know what you need and be able to explain it to the agent so you do not waste time.

Audition every potential model to make sure each fits your label's image and fits in the clothes. Some minor alterations may be needed, but you probably do not want to make major fitting changes to your samples. Keep in mind the garments you want to show, and match your models to the outfits.

The following sample agreement, also found on the accompanying CD, can be used to make sure your models know what you expect. The top part can be filled out by the models. Complete the "engagement information" portion, make a copy for each model, and keep the original for your records.

MODEL AGREEMENT	
Model information	
Name:	
Telephone:	
Address:	
Date of birth:	
Agency:	
Engagement Information	
Description:	
Date:	
Location:	
Associated businesses:	
Contact name:	
Telephone:	
Address:	
Mandatory rehearsals (date, time, location):	
Additional rehearsals (date, time, location):	
Fitting (date, time, location):	
Show call time:	
Show start time:	
Hair instructions for show:	
Makeup instructions for show:	
Other instructions for show:	
Garment return information:	
Payment:	
Model's signature:	Date:_____
Show director's signature:	Date:_____

Consider completing model agreements even if you are using volunteers. Having everything in writing may reduce confusion and encourage participants to treat the fashion show seriously.

Promotional Strategy

Write out how you will bring people to your fashion show. If you are using a location with substantial foot traffic, such as the commons area of a popular mall or park, you may draw a crowd with just a few posters. A more secluded venue may require additional publicity, including direct mailers, press releases, media spots, and flyers at local stores.

Preparing for Your Show

Do you want your audience to see themselves wearing your designs at the beach or at the opera? Do you want to show off the fun color palette of your garments or the sophisticated lines? The music, decorations, and props you select help create the atmosphere of your show.

The emcee who announces the show can also help set the tone of the event. Besides having a good speaking voice, the emcee you choose should have some fashion knowledge and should not be intimidated by speaking in public. Although you should write up a script that describes each fashion and rehearse the show with the models, there may be some delays that require the announcer to improvise. You do not want someone who will get nervous or mispronounce "raglan."

Think about the order you will show your outfits. Each outfit should be connected to the previous one by a design element or inspiration. Even if the link is too subtle for the audience to identify, it will make your show more cohesive.

If your models are mostly volunteers or inexperienced, arrange for several rehearsals so that you can work on timing and walking. These rehearsals do not have to be at the fashion show venue, and they do not have to include every model. They are to help everyone feel comfortable with his or her role and minimize confusion at the show. Rehearsals can also help you identify models that may not be reliable and arrange for understudies. Hair stylists and makeup artists can try out ideas during these practices.

Schedule a full dress rehearsal close to the show. The day before is ideal. Have the rehearsal at the same place the fashion show will be held, with the same audio and lighting equipment, props, decorations, and staff. Try to run through the complete program and make notes of any additional materials you need.

On the day of the show, schedule plenty of time for last-minute clothing alterations. Models will need their hair and makeup done. Have the emcee, models, and stylists arrive early to minimize the worry from late arrivals.

Check that the sound equipment and lights are positioned correctly, even if they are still set up from the previous night's dress rehearsal. One unplugged cord can cause confusion and delay the show.

The hour before the fashion show starts can be a hectic time. Bring a friend or hire an assistant to act as a gofer and help you track down missing accessories, calm nervous models, and run messages to the emcee. If your designs are highly detailed, consider having a seamstress on hand to fix fallen hems and loose seams.

After the Show

Double-check your samples as they are returned. Make sure you get back all the pieces and accessories. Fold or hang the garments, even those that are going to the cleaners.

Leave the venue clean and organized. Put back any furniture that you rearranged. Sweep up the catwalk, dressing room, and audience area. Repack the audio equipment.

Follow up with any buyers or reporters you invited to the show. Ask if they have any questions about your line or need additional information. Send thank you notes to your cohost, emcee, and models. Make sure that you pay any contractors promptly.

FASHION SHOW CHECKLIST

Location

- Location booked
- Show(s) scheduled
- Catwalk, audience section, and dressing rooms laid out

Personnel

- Emcee
- Seamstress
- Lighting technicians
- Makeup artists
- Cleanup crew
- Models
- Audio technicians
- Hair stylists
- Photographer

Equipment

- Sound system
- Seating for audience
- Equipment double-checked morning of show
- Lighting
- Furniture in dressing rooms

Props and Accessories

- Music
- Accessories for each outfit
- Script for emcee
- Accessories for runway

Apparel

- Samples repaired and cleaned
- Samples fitted to models
- Each outfit labeled with model's name
- Each outfit packed with coordinating accessories

FASHION SHOW CHECKLIST

Publicity

- Press releases
- Flyers at local stores
- Follow-up calls to reporters
- Postcards
- Personal calls to buyers

Other

- Snacks and drinks for crew
- Cell phone and local telephone book
- Sewing supplies for emergency repairs and alterations
- Extra extension cords
- Extra batteries

Contact list

- Stopwatch
- Duct tape
- Iron and ironing board
- Extra accessories and two to three extra outfits
- Glue
- Marketing materials
- Steamer

Classes and Workshops

Many people are interested in learning how to look better or create their own clothing. As a design business owner, you can position yourself as the local expert in fashion. Classes and workshops can do more than increase your cash flow. They can help bring potential customers into your studio and increase brand awareness for your label. An innovative class or workshop can be a newsworthy event, which may mean free publicity.

Whether you decide to offer a weekly class or a one-day workshop, there are many topics that may find an audience in your area. For example:

- Sewing your own fashions

- Dressing for your body type

- Combining colors and patterns in your wardrobe

- Accessorizing

- Basic alterations

- Building a professional wardrobe

- Designing your dream wedding gown

- Transitional dressing

- Looking your best at the beach

- Going through pregnancy in style

- Creating a clothing color palette

- Timeless dressing

- How to stay ahead of trends

- Modifying the basic T-shirt

The location you choose for a class will help dictate the overhead expenses, your profit, and the target student. You may choose to hold classes in your own studio or retail space. In this case, any income from tuition may be treated as business income. You will be responsible for marketing your classes, which may be a substantial expense.

If you do not want to market your classes, consider teaching at a recreational center or arts program. Museums, stores, clubs, and libraries may also be interested in hiring an instructor. Colleges may provide continuing education courses. Organizations usually hire teachers as independent contractors who are paid a set fee per hour or per student. You can also teach classes through your local school district's Community Education department or for the school's summer sessions.

The host organization may require you to present a class proposal before hiring you to teach. The proposal is your chance to convince the program director that students would enjoy your class and that you will be a good instructor. The proposal form will ask for information about the purpose of your class, the target market, what materials the students will have to purchase, what topics you will cover, how often and for how long the class will meet, and your experience in the field and as a teacher. Be prepared to provide references.

How you organize your classroom can be a major factor in how well your students learn. A host organization may require a classroom layout as part of a course proposal. The accompanying CD includes some layout ideas for lecture, demonstration, and studio classes.

When you teach your class, treat it as an extension of your design business. Even if your students are unlikely to become clients, they may tell others about their experience in your class. Be professional and organized. Make sure students know what materials they should bring to every class and what they should do to prepare. Use the following checklist, which is also on the accompanying CD, to help organize each class.

CLASS PREPARATION CHECKLIST

- Write out the main goals of the class. What do you hope students will retain after this session?

- Outline an explanation for each of the main goals.

- Prepare at least one demonstration to illustrate a class goal and hold student interest.

CLASS PREPARATION CHECKLIST

- Find examples to illustrate core concepts. Label your examples so you remember which details to point out.

- Make handouts that explain the class goals and include references where students can find more information.

- Plan an assignment that students can complete to demonstrate a mastery of the class goals. You may choose to do the assignment in class or designate it as homework.

- Prepare a list of materials students should bring with them for the next session.

- After the class, make notes about what worked, what questions students raised, and what you want to do differently next time.

Guilds, businesses, and schools may have their own contract for visiting or part-time teachers. If your host organization does not have a standard contract, you may prepare one for its approval. A contract helps make sure that both the teacher and the host understand the expectations.

SAMPLE WORKSHOP AGREEMENT

Name of host organization: _____

Address: _____

Telephone:_____

Name of teacher: _____

Address: _____

Telephone:_____

The above teacher agrees to teach the following workshop:

Name of workshop: _____

Maximum number of students: _____

Date of workshop:_____

SAMPLE WORKSHOP AGREEMENT

Time of workshop:_____

Workshop location:_____

Teacher's fee:_____

Payment to be received:_____

The host agrees to pay the following expenses: _____
_____

The workshop may be canceled by either party no later than _____ calendar days before the above date.

Host's signature: _____

Date:_____

Teacher's signature: _____

Date:_____

Studio Tours and Open Houses

Boutique owners, reporters, and customers may enjoy seeing how you create your designs. A studio tour can help improve your relationship with suppliers and buyers and give you an opportunity to introduce a new style or line.

Your tour can be an invitation-only event, or you can open your workspace to the public. Open houses are more likely to be covered by the press, especially if you will be collecting donations for a local nonprofit organization or offering a free class or service.

Decide who you want to attract to your event, then schedule a day and time that is least likely to interfere with your visitors' work schedule or personal responsibilities. Before holding a tour or open house, make sure that your studio is tidy. Any equipment should be put away, unplugged, or locked to reduce the risk of accidents. Put out sample garments and storyboards for your visitors to look at and touch. Consider providing light refreshments to put guests in a better mood. Have plenty of marketing materials on hand, and make sure that all visitors leave with a business card, catalog, or brochure.

Charity Events

Some consumers identify with the goals of the nonprofit organizations their money supports, so participating in a charity event can help brand your business. A design company with an image of being "green" can support that image by raising money for environmental causes. On the other hand, a tennis skirt designer may benefit from supporting a charity that encourages girls to participate in sports.

Businesses have different reasons for including charitable activities in their public relations plans. Some may find that a large percentage of supporters of a particular cause are part of their target market. Others may want to be involved with a high-profile event that will be covered in the media.

Possible charitable activities that may help market your business include:

- Donating apparel or a gift certificate to a raffle that benefits a nonprofit organization.

- Hosting a fashion show with an entrance fee that goes to a charity.

- Donating last season's samples to a clothes closet.

- Auctioning custom garments to benefit a cause.

- Donating part of the proceeds from a particular design.

✦ Licensing the trademark of a cause or organization and including it on apparel.

✦ Designing costumes for a local theater production.

Personal Appearances

Once you have placed your fashions at a boutique or other retail business, arrange to make a personal visit to the store. A guest appearance can have many benefits. You will have the opportunity to meet the sales staff and explain to them what sets your garments apart from the competition. The store owner will likely be pleased to host your visit as a low cost public relations event.

Besides improving your relationship with retailers, personal appearances can help build brand recognition. Customers are likely to remember the name of the fashion designer they shook hands with at their favorite dress shop. Local media may want to cover your appearance, especially if your line is doing well at the store or if you are from out of town.

Always have a few nice things to say about the town and store you are visiting, even if you are disappointed with the location or how the store is marketing your designs. A sarcastic or poorly worded quote in the local paper may sour your business relationship. Treat the sales staff like royalty. Not only can they nudge customers toward your apparel, but in the future they may work at different stores or even operate their own boutiques. If they remember you as a friendly person to work with, you may find it easier to get future sales contracts.

Personal Appearance Checklist

🌢 Set a budget for your appearance.

🌢 Arrange a date and time for the appearance with the owner of the host store. Try to stay all day or make multiple appearances throughout a weekend to reach the most customers.

🌢 Plan your traveling and overnight accommodations, if required. Larger stores may underwrite your visit, but smaller retailers may expect you to pay your own expenses.

🌢 With the store owner, develop a marketing plan for your appearance.

🌢 Write a press release announcing your appearance. Add it to your media kit and distribute it to the local newspapers and television news programs.

🌢 Distribute a flyer announcing your appearance at the store.

🌢 Design a postcard to be mailed to the store's regular customers.

🌢 With the store owner, write an itinerary for the visit. You may want to schedule a tour of the store or town, a meal with the sales staff, a reception with special customers, or other events.

🌢 Follow up with reporters. Offer to schedule interviews or private showings of your line while you are in town.

🌢 Organize gifts for your host and the sales staff. Clothing or accessories from your line are good choices.

🌢 If you have any samples ready for your next season's line, bring them and offer the store owner a special "sneak peek."

Legal Considerations of Special Events

A fashion show, trunk show, workshop, or personal appearance can be a fun and profitable break from the everyday rigors of running a business. Because these events are out of the ordinary, you may find there are special regulations that apply.

Before hosting any event, check with your insurance provider to make sure you are covered against accidents, injuries, and property loss or damage. If you usually do not have visitors or employees in your studio, your insurance policy may not cover an open house or workshop. Consider purchasing a temporary rider to protect you in case an attendee gets hurt at the event.

You may also need to apply for a special license or permit, especially if you do not retail your own designs but will be hosting a retail event. Contact your local or state commerce department for more information.

If you will be holding an event off your own premises, make sure the contract addresses the possibility of the venue becoming unavailable or you decide to back out. Negotiate who will pay for the printing and distribution of new advertisements and under what circumstances the deposit is refundable.

If you are holding an event to benefit a nonprofit organization, there may be limitations to what you can say in your advertisements. Let an attorney, either yours or the organization's, review any marketing material before it is distributed. There may also be local regulations about who can control what parts of the event. For example, your company may not be able to hold a raffle on behalf of a nonprofit organization, but you could donate money or merchandise directly to the organization for use as prizes in a raffle. Work with the nonprofit organization, your local government, and your lawyer to make sure your charitable event follows all applicable laws.

If you plan to sell directly to consumers at a personal appearance, workshop, or fashion show, make sure the hosting business or organization approves. Negotiate what percentage of the total sales income the host should receive. The host may prefer to handle transactions through his or her cash register. If that is the case, make sure the customers know who to contact in case they need to return a garment. A store that carries your current line may want you to sell only samples or discontinued styles. Make sure you are not breaking any exclusivity agreements you have signed with retailers.

Cost Considerations of Special Events

Hosting a special event can be a major business expense. In addition to renting a venue and purchasing additional insurance, you may need to hire assistants to keep the event moving smoothly. You may need to have additional samples or merchandise constructed or have apparel cleaned, repaired, or altered.

Estimate your travel expenses, including preparation trips to research possible venues. If you are hosting a class or workshop, list the materials you will provide to students. If you have a loyal clientele, word of mouth advertising may be enough to fill up the seats at your event. Less-established companies should budget for designing, printing, and mailing marketing materials. Decide what kind and how many advertisements in the local media you can afford to purchase.

Media Relations

The media can be a fashion designer's best friend or worst enemy. A glowing review by a fashion writer may make demand for your styles explode. A report in the business section that alludes to financial insecurity or irresponsibility may make a retail store leery about placing an order. An article in the life style section about your company's involvement with a local charity helps shape your image.

A press release is a way of announcing changes and events to the media. Reporters are looking for good stories, but most do not want to be bombarded with press releases that are not newsworthy.

Before sending a press release, determine which department or reporter would be the best match for the story. Some publications have a directory on their Web sites or editorial pages. You may want to read several issues of the publication to get a feel for how news is divided among the sections.

Even if you target the right reporter, a press release may be ignored if it does not follow a standard format. Put your contact information in the upper left hand corner of the paper. Underneath or beside that, type the date the information should be published or, "FOR IMMEDIATE RELEASE."

Below that, write a short title for the article. This title should be capitalized and centered. On the next line you can add a more descriptive subtitle. Signal the end of the press release by typing, "# # #" or, "-END-." At the bottom of the paper, let the reporter know how to get in touch with you for an interview.

In the body of the press release, be sure to include the relevant facts about the event: where and when it will be, how much it will cost, and who is invited. Newspapers may publish press releases as written, so add some quotes to make the release readable and interesting.

Keep your press release short and to the point. If the reporter wants to expand the story, he or she will arrange an interview. Do not put in so much information about your business that the event information is lost. If you prefer, you can add a section to the end of the press release that describes your professional experience. Before sending a press release, make sure your contact information is current and easy to find.

A good press release may lead to a more extensive article or a feature story. It can also help you become known in the press as a local fashion expert. If reporters need information for a future story, they may contact you. Building a relationship with the press can help you get the publicity you need to make your special events successful.

The sample press release below, also found on the accompanying CD, shows a standard press release format.

SAMPLE PRESS RELEASE

Contact: Peter Sampson
Phone: (999) 999-9999
E-mail: p.sampson@yourdesignbusiness.com

FOR IMMEDIATE RELEASE

DESIGNER HOSTS WEDDING TRENDS SHOW
White Hills Mall Event Benefits Veterans

Local brides will have the chance to see the latest styles of wedding gowns, jewelry, tuxedoes, and flower arrangements during a free event at the White Hills Mall.

Designer Peter Sampson will be hosting a wedding fashion show on December 1 at the White Hills Mall. The show will feature Sampson's gowns in addition to jewelry from Silversmith's Diamonds and flowers from Carey Floral Masters.

"Both Silversmith's Diamonds and Carey Floral are known for their cutting-edge designs," Sampson says. "We are thrilled to be able to show women the kind of styles that are being seen in Paris and New York this winter."

Sampson has been designing custom wedding gowns since 1999. "Women want to look beautiful and timeless on their wedding day," he says. "I help make their dream dresses become reality."

SAMPLE PRESS RELEASE

Refreshments for the event will be provided by the White Hills Veterans Association, a 501(c) nonprofit organization. Donations for a scholarship fund for children of veterans will be accepted at the event.

"The White Hills Veterans Association has been helping our soldiers and their families since 1958," says Sampson. "It is an honor to be able to help them."

The fashion show will be held December 1, at noon in the White Hills Mall main plaza.

#

For more information or to schedule an interview, please contact Peter Sampson at (999) 999-9999 or e-mail p.sampson@yourdesignbusiness.com

CASE STUDY: JANE THORNLEY JEWELRY AND KNITWEAR DESIGN

Jane Thornley, Owner
Jane Thornley Jewelry and Knitwear Design
www.janethornley.com

I began my business by selling scarves at a local artisan show. I started selling other garments, and they sold well, too. Now I sell my knits through shows, galleries, and Internet sites. People seemed to like my garments, so I began selling my patterns on my Web site.

After 30 years working in education, I retired last year. I decided to combine my love of traveling, knitting, and meeting new people by arranging tours that combine workshops, tours, and meeting local artisans. The tours are for anyone interested in design.

I tell my students that I hope they will never be the same after one of my workshops. I want them to feel comfortable playing with colors and textures and not feel locked in by a pattern.

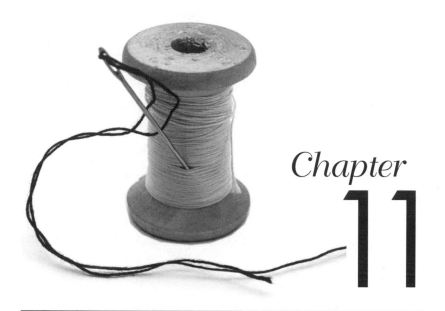

Chapter

11

Accounting &
Bookkeeping

*A*s a business owner, you need to keep accurate financial records. Not only are you legally obligated to have the documentation to support any tax statements you file, but you also need correct and up-to-date information to analyze the health of your operations and the effectiveness of your marketing strategies.

IRS Requirements

The IRS requires you be able to prove what expenses are business-related. After you file a tax statement, you should keep the supporting financial papers at least until the statute of limitations for that return expires. The statute of limitations for tax statements may be up to seven years after the return is due or two years after it was paid, whichever is later.

You may need to save your receipts, invoices, canceled checks, sales slips, and deposit tickets in case a statement is questioned by the IRS. In addition, a log of travel, entertainment, and business gift expenses can help support the information you give on your tax forms. A business expense log should list the price, time, place, and purpose of each transaction. In addition, if the transaction involved someone else, list your business relationship. For example, if you took someone out to lunch to discuss your designs, you need to indicate if he or she was a client, seamstress, model, supplier, or manufacturer.

The following records should be saved as supporting documents for your tax statements:

- Business checking account register

- Depreciation worksheets

- Employee time sheets

- Payroll records

- Monthly and daily summaries of cash receipts

- Invoices

- Sales receipts

- Travel and entertainment log

- Appraisal records

- Estimated tax statements

- Canceled checks

- Deposit tickets

Who Should Keep the Books?

Some business owners choose to manage their own accounting records to save the expense of hiring a bookkeeper. However, if you do not have the necessary skills, you may end up making costly mistakes. In addition, you may find that bookkeeping takes up time you would rather devote to designing or promoting your line.

If you would rather pay a professional to track your income and expenses, you can choose to hire a full- or part-time employee, contract with an accounting business, or use a freelance bookkeeper.

The major benefit to hiring a bookkeeper is convenience. There may be times when you need a detailed financial report or a specific question answered. If you have a skilled financial professional on staff, you may find it quicker and easier to get the information you need. By hiring your own bookkeeper, you also have the opportunity to check applicants' references and experience to help assure that the person balancing your books is reliable and capable.

Hiring a bookkeeper, even part-time, can be expensive. Unless you understand the system your bookkeeper uses, you are at his or her mercy. You may not recognize if money is missing or if the financial health of your business is declining. If the bookkeeper is not trustworthy, you may lose significant amounts of money.

Using an accounting or bookkeeping service is often less expensive than hiring an employee. In addition, a firm often has safeguard methods in place to reduce errors and fraud. The drawback to using an outside service is convenience. You may have to wait for reports and statements.

A freelance bookkeeper can be the least expensive choice, short of handling the books yourself. Unlike an accounting firm, a freelancer probably does not have multiple people checking the calculations. This can increase the risk of errors or fraud. A freelance bookkeeper's schedule may vary from week to week. He or she may not be available to create reports or update your records when you need them.

Bookkeeping and Financial Analysis

When you first start your business, you may make predictions based on your market research. By studying your books as your business grows, you can see where reality does not mesh with projections. You can see where you are overspending and what products are performing better than anticipated. Accurate accounts help you detect spending and income trends within your business, which can help you make better estimates for future performance.

Your financial books are the pulse of your business. Analyzing your performance helps you know when to look for additional financing and when you can afford to invest in newer equipment.

Reviewing your books can help you see how money flows out of your business and control overspending. There are three main types of expenses that your fashion design business may have. Direct expenses are those that are spent entirely on the business. The cost of office supplies, labels, and fabric are direct expenses. Capital expenses are those that benefit the business over a long time, such as manufacturing equipment or real estate. Prorated expenses can only be partially attributed to the business. For example, if your studio is in your home, then your mortgage payment may be a prorated expense. As a business owner, you should keep track of all three types of expenses to make sure you are not overspending your income.

Bookkeeping and Marketing Analysis

Analyzing your income and expenses can help you understand which marketing campaigns are working and which have poor returns on investment. A sudden spike in sales after a direct mailing can indicate that you reached your target market. The change in sales the weeks after a special event can help you evaluate the success of the event.

You may benefit from running periodic sales reports to see how different designs are selling. Check with any retailers selling your fashions and compare performances. Customers in different areas may have different tastes, but a particularly low sales report may indicate that a store does not attract your target market or is not effectively displaying your garments.

Financial analyses can reveal more than problems. A visit to a store where your designs are selling well might yield some marketing and sales strategies that could improve your line's performance at other retailers. Keeping track of what designs become your best-sellers each season can give you valuable insight into what your target market wants. Charting how raising or dropping prices on individual styles affects sales can help you focus your pricing strategy.

Handling Transactions

As part of a good bookkeeping policy, you should keep a record of every monetary transaction. The types of financial transactions you need to handle depend on whether you sell your garments to retailers, consumers, or both.

Retail customers expect to pay for their purchases using cash, checks, credit cards, or debit cards. Each of these payment methods has potential risk to retailers. Cash can be counterfeited, checks may bounce, and credit or debit cards may be stolen. There are some practical ways to reduce losses from fraudulent transactions: ask your banker to help you identify counterfeit bills, make sure the contact information on any check you accept is current and use a check verification service, and require photo identification before accepting a check or debit card.

In addition to cash, checks, and cards, you may need to record returns and store credit transactions. Make sure to keep detailed records of each retail transaction. You should log the date and amount of each retail sale as well as the style, size, and quantity of every piece sold. Accurate records will help you track your inventory and analyze sales trends.

If you sell your designs wholesale, you are less likely to encounter cash transactions. If a buyer pays in cash, make sure to issue a comprehensive receipt and to keep a copy as a record of the purchase.

Small chains and independent stores may pay for merchandise with checks or credit cards. Department stores and larger chains are more likely to order on credit. Do not be afraid of offending a buyer by running a credit check before signing a contract that requires you to accept credit.

Payroll and Taxes

If you have any employees, you will need to keep accurate payroll records. Business accounting software that helps automate payroll recordkeeping is available, but you can also track employees' work records by hand. Either way, calculating payroll daily can help reduce disagreements, errors, and misreporting. Reviewing employee records each day can also help you recognize if you are under or overstaffed.

As an employer, it is your responsibility to calculate, withhold, and pay income tax, Social Security, Medicare, and federal unemployment taxes for your employees. Businesses usually pay estimated taxes throughout the year and file their taxes once a year. If you are a sole proprietorship with no employees, you can file your business income and expenses with your personal taxes. Partnerships file an "information return" rather than a tax return.

In addition to income tax on your business earnings, you may have to pay federal self-employment tax. Self-employment tax allows people who work for themselves to pay into Social Security and Medicare.

State, city, and county tax reporting requirements vary. Check with your local government office to see what forms you must file.

If you are operating your fashion design business from your home, you may be entitled to deduct part of your housing expenses when filing your federal taxes. Years ago, claiming the home business use deduction was thought to be inviting an audit. Now that telecommuting and home-based businesses have become more prevalent, the business use of the home deduction has become more widespread.

You may qualify for the business use of the home deduction if you set aside part of your home specifically for your business and if that space is your primary place of business. Even if you do not have a dedicated space for your business operations, you may qualify for the deduction if you regularly store your samples or inventory in your home, as long as your home is the only fixed place you operate your business from and you store your merchandise in a separate and identifiable area.

If you qualify for the home business use deduction, you may be entitled to deduct a percentage of your real estate taxes, mortgage interest, depreciation, insurance, utilities, repairs, and rent. The percentage you can deduct depends on the type of expense, the size of your home, and the amount of your home you use for your business operations. If you renovate, repair, or redecorate the areas used exclusively for your business, those costs may be completely deductible.

CASE STUDY: MOUNTAIN MAMA ORIGINALS

Susanna Evins, Owner
Mountain Mama Originals
www.mountainmamaoriginals.
wordpress.com

Sewing has been a lifelong hobby for me, including designing and stitching clothes for local shows and events. Yet it was not until our first daughter was born that I tried to make it into a business. I bought a new sewing machine and really started playing around with designing appliqués and patterns.

I begin every creation by designing an appliqué, and then I choose the colors of dyes and threads to make the piece really "pop." As a self-taught seamstress, I use simple patterns and am constantly improving my sewing skills, but the vibrant and unique appliqués are what make my clothing come alive. Usually, I take a scene out of nature and capture the color, lighting, and mood of the beauty. I then choose the weight and texture of the fabric for each piece.

All my fabric is made from organic hemp blends. I chose hemp because it is one of the strongest and most durable of all natural textile fibers. Products made from hemp will outlast their competition by many years. Not only is hemp strong, but it also holds its shape, stretching less than any other natural fiber. This prevents hemp garments from becoming distorted with use. I want my creations to last, not for a year, but for many years. Many times I have purchased clothing off the rack, and it has fallen apart within three to six months — sometimes sooner.

Hemp may be known for its durability, but its comfort and style are second to none. The more hemp is used, the softer it gets. Hemp does not wear out; it wears in. Hemp is also naturally resistant to mold and ultraviolet light. Due to the porous nature of the fiber, hemp is more water absorbent and will dye and retain its color better than any fabric, including cotton. This porous nature allows hemp to "breathe," so that it is cool in warm weather. Furthermore, air, which is trapped in the fibers, is warmed by the body, making hemp garments naturally warm in cooler weather.

CASE STUDY: MOUNTAIN MAMA ORIGINALS

I pursued fashion design to let my emotions and vision of life be expressed as art — and not just art on a wall but functional and comfortable art that can be worn and loved. I wanted to provide one-of-a-kind, quality clothing and to make others feel special in a personal way. Every girl I know loves to look pretty and to stand out from the rest of the pack. In past generations, people would have their measurements taken; choose their pattern, fabric, ribbons, and possibly beads; and then have the dress made. Today, we have accepted that our clothing comes off a rack. We think custom-made clothing is not available without paying a pretty penny. I provide a piece that screams, "YOU," for a reasonable price. When you put on one of my designs, you feel like you are not just one of the pack.

Over the past three years, I have learned much about being successful at business: I do my research, see what styles are out there and change them to fit my unique design, make sure that I am always standing out of the crowd, and appreciate and learn from the very talented women online selling their creations. We are a sisterhood. We need to support, encourage, and never duplicate others' work. Our designs come from our soul, and we all have the ability to amaze ourselves.

Customer service is absolutely vital. I communicate, make sure my customers know I am listening, and share in their excitement for the creation. They are thrilled to have a piece customized for them that shows the world their personality. What is more, I have been surprised at how many of my customers have become personal friends. I was not looking for that, but I find it to be the most rewarding part of business.

Many people ask me how I find the time to sew with two active girls under the age of four. Like everyone else, I make time for it, just as some people make time for their favorite TV shows or a book they are reading. A typical day consists of caring for my two girls, going for bike rides and walks with them, and tidying up the house. As soon as nap time rolls around, it is off to sewing. I usually sew three or four hours a day during the week and five to eight hours on the weekend. I love what I do, and I feel extremely lucky to have this opportunity.

I have a loving, close-knit family. My husband is a science/math teacher and a wonderful husband and father. We are lucky in the summertime to have daddy

CASE STUDY: MOUNTAIN MAMA ORIGINALS

home for three months. My daughters are true angels. They often inspire me and infuse my life with joy. I have a business that inspires me with designs and infuses my life with joy. I have a business that fulfills me. I am captivated by the energy and colors of life, which I feel is seen in my work.

Through my business you can order a custom piece that will be worn for years and will never be dated — because it is you.

Chapter

12

Budgeting &
Operational
Management

A successful fashion business needs to keep a close eye on its cash flow. Cash flow is a measure of all the money that is received and spent by the business.

Creating a working budget is a way of planning your estimated cash flow. A working budget will give you a good idea of how much money you should expect to pay in expenses and receive in sales or financing from month to month. Knowing how to earmark your funds will help you calculate how much you can spend on your samples and save for equipment purchases. There may be a significant time between when you deliver an order and when you are paid, especially when working with major department stores. A budget can help you prepare for these periods of low cash flow.

Operational Expenses

The funds paid out to keep a business running are a major budget consideration. These operational expenses may include rent, supplies, services, labor, marketing, supplies, depreciation, and utilities.

Rent

Unless you work in your home, you may need to rent studio space, an office where you can meet with clients, storage facilities for manufactured garments, or a retail area. Even if you do operate your business from your house or apartment, you may need to allocate funds for showcase space rental.

In the short term, you may find it more cost effective to rent rather than buy expensive equipment, such as sewing and knitting machines. Analyzing your rental budget can help you determine at which point purchasing the equipment makes financial sense.

Supplies

Supplies are noninventory goods that are replaced frequently, such as printer toner, pattern paper, and display boards.

Budgeting for your supplies can reduce impulsive or frivolous purchases. You can reduce the expense of supplies by buying in bulk and looking for deals such as free shipping with a minimum purchase. If you do not use enough of a specific supply to justify buying in bulk, consider sharing a purchase with another business.

Services

If you use a lawyer, accountant, seamstress, or patternmaker, include the fees in your budget. Fashion design businesses that often use samples for trunk or fashion shows may need to budget extra money for garment dry cleaning, alterations, and repairs.

If you keep expensive materials, inventory, or samples on your premises, or if your business is located in an area with a high crime rate, you may want to budget for a security service.

Sewing equipment should receive regular maintenance to reduce the risk of costly repairs. When developing your operational expenses budget, check with your dealer for the recommended schedule and approximate cost of maintenance.

Shipping is another common service used by a fashion design business. The faster you need a shipment, the more you should expect to pay. Reduce shipping costs by planning your material needs early and using slower but more economical methods. Shipping providers and common carrier services have different rate schedules based on origin, weight, shape, and destination of the package, so it may pay to shop around for the best deal each time you have a large shipment.

Retail stores may have set policies about what method of shipping should be used and who should pay. If you are selling wholesale, review your contract thoroughly to make sure you can budget the shipping costs. If the shipping seems excessive, contact your buyer to see if you can use a substitute carrier. Be aware that if you use a different shipping method than specified in a sales contract without authorization from your buyer, you risk having the purchase canceled.

You may be able to reduce you services expenses by bartering with other businesses. Bartering is the direct exchange of goods or services. For example, if you are a skilled patternmaker, you may be able to barter patternmaking services to another designer in exchange for sewing, modeling, or materials.

Training

In the fashion industry, there are always new skills to learn. If you or an employee plan on taking classes to improve your sewing technique, learn about accounting, or improve your sales skills, be sure to include the cost of tuition, travel, and supplies in your budget.

Labor

For a new fashion design business, labor is not likely to be a major expense. However, as your business grows, you may need to hire a bookkeeper, assistant, seamstress, illustrator, or sales representative.

There are three types of labor expenses. Monthly salaries are fixed amounts usually paid to full-time staff members. Hourly wages are used for part-time employees. The labor cost in hourly wages may vary significantly according to a fashion business's production cycle. Overtime expenses are those paid in addition to regularly hourly wages.

The Federal Labor Standards Act requires that employees pay workers 150 percent their usual hourly rate for any hours worked after the first 40 in a week. Your business may be affected by additional local regulations.

Because overtime labor expenses can add up quickly, it is important to keep an eye on work schedules, especially when preparing for a fashion show or filling a large order.

Depreciation

Depreciation is a measure of the decreased value of an asset. To claim depreciation as a business expense, you must own the asset and use it in your business. In addition, the asset must have a determinable lifespan in terms of usefulness and be expected to last longer than a year. Vehicles, real estate, manufacturing equipment, and computers are examples of assets that depreciate.

The IRS sets standards for the rates of depreciation you can claim on your tax statements. IRS Publication 946, which is included on the accompanying CD, details how to calculate depreciation.

Marketing

Marketing can include any activity that helps promote your designs. Whether you sell garments to retailers or directly to consumers, marketing can help educate your buyers about what sets your clothing apart from the competition.

When setting your marketing budget, think about what methods you are going to use, how often you are going to run each type of strategy, and how long each campaign will last. Your marketing budget may include other types of operating expenses. For example, you may decide to use a marketing consultant to help you create your strategies or a graphic artist to design flyers. Both of these are services. If you print flyers you will need to budget for paper and toner, which are supplies.

Maintenance and Repairs

Sewing equipment should receive regular maintenance to reduce the risk of costly repairs. When developing your operational expenses budget, check with your dealer for the recommended schedule and approximate cost of maintenance.

Complicated manufacturing machines may have predictable repair schedules. Talk to your dealer or search the Internet for other people who use the same model to get an idea of how often you should expect to need specific repairs so that you can budget appropriately.

Utilities

Electricity, gas, telephone, Internet, and water service may billed monthly. If you live in a place with seasonal weather fluctuations, your utility bills may vary from month to month. Some utility providers offer budget plans that equalize the payments throughout the year.

Charitable Contributions

Donating money or gifts can help enhance your business's image and increase your name recognition. Charitable contributions to organizations that appeal to your target market can be an effective marketing technique.

Unlike other expenses like rent and utilities, you get to decide how often and how much you want to budget for charity.

Insurance

Business and property insurance payments may be monthly, quarterly, semiannually, or yearly. Your insurance company may charge a small fee for the convenience of dividing the premium into smaller payments.

Taxes

Your business may be subject to state, local, federal, property, and labor taxes. Most businesses are required to pay estimated taxes quarterly and file tax statements annually. If you find that you owe more than you have paid in estimated taxes, you will have to pay the balance when you file your statement. If you have overpaid your taxes, you can elect to receive a refund of the balance or apply the balance to the next year's taxes.

Packaging

If you retail your designs, you can choose how you wish to package your garments. If you sell your designs to retail stores, however, they may have strict labeling and packaging requirements. A department store chain may want each shirt folded around a pasteboard form and bagged or that slacks arrive on wooden hangers. Following these guidelines can be costly, but if you choose to ignore the instructions, you may have the entire shipment sent back to you at your expense.

Loan Repayment

If you obtained a business loan to start your business or to purchase equipment, your operational expenses will include your loan payments. Credit card payments are also considered loan repayments.

Bad Debt

Bad debt refers to bounced checks, unpaid credit, and fraudulent credit card transactions. Although there are legal channels to recover funds lost through bad debt, it may take months for the issue to be resolved. It is better for your cash flow to avoid bad debt as much as possible. Ask for identification before accepting checks or credit cards, and review a buyer's credit history before shipping large orders on credit.

Revenue

When starting your fashion design business, it may be more difficult to estimate your revenue than your expenses. It is better to use conservative income numbers when writing your budget, as it is easier to deal with excess revenue than a shortfall.

Most of the revenue in your budget will likely come from retail or wholesale purchases, but your business may have other types of income streams.

Retail Sales

Retail sales come through several channels. Some purchases may be made in person at trunk sales or your retail location. Customers may place orders through the mail after reviewing your catalog. Commissioned pieces may be purchased over the telephone. Visitors to your Web site may order designs over the Internet.

If you decide to sell you creations directly to the consumer, have a system in place to keep track of what people purchase, how they order, and by what method they pay. This will help you compare and analyze different rates and budget more effectively in the future.

Wholesale Revenue

It is possible to build a successful fashion design business without ever making retail sales yourself. Wholesale revenue often comes as the result of personal contact. For independent stores, the personal contact may be a sales call to the store owner or manager. Fashion designers may connect with buyers for department stores at market weeks, trade shows, or market center showcases.

You may sell to retail stores yourself or through a sales representative. If you use a sales representative, remember to budget for his or her percentage of the gross purchase price.

Keep thorough records of your sales contacts, including how you met and how the sales were made. This will help you budget more accurately and efficiently. For example, if you find that most your sales were the result of meetings at a trade show and few were from your market center showcase, you may divert next season's funds from the showcase rental to attend an additional trade show. If you find that your sales representative generates more orders than you do, you may find it more cost effective to stay in the studio and work on your designs while your representative attends the next market week.

Other Revenue

If you plan to offer services or classes, be sure to include your estimated intake in your operational budget. Some of the skills you may have developed in preparation for operating your fashion design business may be marketable themselves. In addition to supplementing your business income during slow periods, additional streams of revenue can help you become more firmly established in the fashion industry. Some of the ways you may bring more money into your business include:

- Garment alterations

- Teaching

- Patternmaking

- Sample construction

- Fashion drawing

- Fashion show management

Monthly Budgeting

A fashion design business is likely to have different budget needs from month to month. Some months will include material purchase and manufacturing costs while others may include travel expenses and trade shows. Because of standard wholesale purchase contracts, you may find that your payments from retail chains occur in three or four clusters throughout the year.

It may not be realistic to try to stabilize cash flow throughout the year, but you should try to plan for months when you expect your expenses to exceed your income.

Analyzing and Using the Numbers

The fashion industry tends to be cyclical. With experience, you will get a better feel for how your budget numbers change throughout the year. Two key financial indicators are net profit and profit margin.

Net profit refers to the sum of the income from all revenue streams over a specific time minus the sum of all operational expenses. Checking your net profit often will let you see when expenses have overwhelmed your income.

Sales growth is often gauged by profit margin. Profit margin is the purchase price for a garment or design minus the cost of bringing that item to market. Couture designers tend to sell a few designs at a high profit margin. At the other end of the spectrum are designers who wholesale T-shirts to major department store chains that may sell hundreds of thousands of units. Each shirt may have a profit margin of only a few cents.

As your business grows and you sell more designs, you may be able to take advantage of bulk material pricing or manufacturing rates. You may also become more efficient at the design, sales, and manufacturing process. All these should help your profit margin.

Tracking Sales Trends

Accurate and complete income records can help you determine which designs are selling and what sales strategies are working. This can help you increase revenue in the future by investing more money in effective marketing campaigns.

Analyzing sales data can help you develop a better understanding of the members of your target market, including how much they prefer to spend on clothing, what styles of clothing they prefer, and features they look for in garments. This understanding can help you decrease your future expenses by cutting designs that are less likely to sell from your line before they reach the sample-making stage.

Budget Deficits

Whenever your actual operational expenses exceed what you projected, you should try to determine the causes. An unexpected event may require additional services or materials. If you overspent your budget in one or several categories, decide if you will be able to reduce your costs in the future or if you need to update your budget for upcoming months.

A budget deficit may be the result of lower than expected income. If your revenue projections were higher than your actual performance, it may be due to one of the following causes:

- You are not investing enough time or money in marketing your designs.

- Your marketing strategy is not effectively reaching your target market.

- The price of your designs is not attractive to your target market. For some markets, the cheapest price is not necessarily the best.

- You are not differentiating yourself enough from other designers who sell to your potential customers.

Reconsidering your pricing and marketing strategies may help increase your revenue and lower your budget deficit. Tapping additional revenue streams, such as providing a service, introducing a line that is targeted to a different market, or teaching a class, may also improve your cash flow.

Chapter
13

Using Technology

---

*T*echnology can help you run your fashion design business more efficiently. With a Web site, you can reach potential customers across the world. Computer programs make it easier to keep your books and run payroll. E-mail allows you to communicate with buyers quickly and inexpensively.

Your Business Web site and E-mail

Depending on your target market, you may need a business Web site. A Web site can have many functions. You can use it to showcase your fashions, facilitate retail or wholesale purchases, communicate with buyers, publicize your line, or create an image. Consumers and buyers may look at your Web site to see if your business looks legitimate before completing a purchase. A well-designed site can reassure them that you are a professional and will complete your contract obligations. A Web site that looks amateurish and thrown together may brand you as a hobbyist and make them hesitant to buy your designs.

Do You Need a Business Web site and E-mail Address?

Not every fashion design business needs a Web site. If you complete most of your deals at trade events or on personal sales visits, you may find that you can operate your business without an online presence.

You may find a Web site helps your business if:

- You sell your designs retail.

- You plan on developing repeat customers.

- Your line changes often.

- You want to communicate directly to your target market.

- You have frequent sales promotions and special events.

- You have special expertise or knowledge that would appeal to your target market.

E-mail allows to you communicate with buyers, suppliers, and service providers without long-distance telephone expenses. If you have a question about a fabric or shipment, you can e-mail your contact directly. Otherwise, you may have to wait until your contact is in the office and free to take your call.

Even if you have an e-mail address that you use for socializing or for your day job, consider getting an address to use specifically for your business. A dedicated e-mail address can help you keep your fashion-related correspondence organized.

When choosing a professional e-mail address, select one that is simple to spell and easy to remember. Avoid free e-mail services that attach advertisements to your e-mails, as they can be irritating to the recipients and make your operation look amateurish.

Some businesses have separate addresses for orders, inquiries, billings, and customer service. The e-mail service you select should provide enough addresses to keep your operations organized and allow for growth. Consider the reliability of the service, and review any file transfer and business use restrictions. Some services charge extra for technical support. Others offer free Web-based access that allows you to check your e-mail from any computer that is connected to the Internet. E-mail services also differ in how much storage space they provide.

Securing a Domain and E-mail Address

A domain name is the letters and numbers, followed by an extension such as ".com" or ".org," that serves as your Web site's address on the Internet.

A good domain name is simple, memorable, and unique. An overly complicated address might be hard for customers to remember. An address that is too similar to another site's might cause lost sales due to typing errors.

You may be able to register a domain name through your Internet service provider, but other companies may offer better rates. The International Corporation for Assigned Names and Numbers (ICANN) maintains a list of accredited Web site registrars at **www.icann.org**.

Your preferred address may already be taken, so make a list of several choices. Despite the availability of other extensions, many people equate ".com" with business Web sites. Customers may have a more difficult time remembering and finding your Web site if you use a different extension, such as ".biz" or ".us."

If you cannot register any of your first choices of domain names, consider using some of the following:

- A word related to your target market, followed by "fashion" or your business name

- Your name by itself or followed by "designs" or "studio"

- "FashionsBy" your business name

- "DesignsFor" your target market

- A phrase that describes your design aesthetic

Creating a Web site

Unless you have an Web server, you will need to contract with a service to host your Web site and allow others to access it over the Internet.

Web site hosting services can vary from free plans to those that cost several hundred dollars per month, but price is not the only consideration. Some Web site hosts provide special software, such as shopping and Web site design utilities, that may save businesses money over the long term. Free services often display advertisements on hosted Web sites or limit the types of files that are supported.

Before signing a service agreement, research the reliability and reputation of the Web site host. If you plan on using several pictures of your designs, a fast server may be a high priority. Internet users tend to have little patience with sites that take too long to load. If your Web site is on a slow server, you will find potential customers clicking away from your site before they have a chance to see your garments.

If you intend to complete sales over the Internet, make sure that you use a service with the most up-to-date high-level security features available in order to protect your customers' identity and credit card information. Even if you are not going to sell over the Internet, make sure your Web site is protected from viruses and unauthorized access.

Templates and Custom Web sites

When building your Web site, you may use ready-made templates or have a custom site designed. Many templates allow you to manipulate graphics and move elements in order to create a more personalized site. They may be cheaper than hiring a professional to create a custom site, but it may be difficult to find a single template that has the look and functionality you need.

What to Include

The goals you have for your Web site determine what you should include. If you want to draw in your target market, either to make sales or to increase brand recognition, consider including features that would appeal to it. These features may include articles, utilities, discussion boards, pictures, chat rooms, and blogs.

Articles can help visitors find your Web site through Internet searches. Even if they come to your site looking for information, if they see a design they like, the visit might end with a purchase. To be most effective, use articles that are informative, well-written, and unique. You do not have to limit your topics to fashion. If you design tennis outfits, articles about the perfect serve or reviews of tournaments might help drive your target market to your site. If you do not have the time, skills, or inclination, a writing professional can help build content.

Utilities include games, calculators, planners, and other applications that visitors to your Web site might find useful. You may want to include a graphic utility that helps visitors visualize what your fashions might look like on their body type or a program that allows them to experiment with different colors and patterns before placing a custom order. You can purchase templates for common types of Web site utilities or hire a computer programmer to design unique programs for your site.

Discussion boards or forums may not only bring your target market to your site, but also encourage repeat visits. An active discussion board helps build content for your site, which in turn brings more visitors and potential buyers. To help your board grow, take part in the discussions yourself. Try to make sure the threads are up to date and filled with useful information. Consider using a "pay per post" service to help encourage dialog on your forum.

The graphics on your Web site can help build consumer excitement about your fashions. Think of your Web site as a combination of a look book and catalog. Use pictures that show off your aesthetic and image as much as your designs.

Chat rooms, like discussion boards, allow visitors to become part of your online presence. Unlike discussion boards, chat rooms are real-time conversations between participants. This offers fashion design business owners the opportunity to schedule virtual special events such as interviews, workshops, and classes, without much overhead.

A blog, or online journal, about issues relevant to your target market is another way to encourage repeat visits to your Web site. To create an effective blog, update it regularly and interact with visitors who post their opinions on your entries.

In addition to features designed to draw in traffic from your target market, consider adding some of the following information to help visitors find information about your business:

- Contact information

- Design philosophy

- Return and shipping policies

- Employment opportunities

- Business history

Online Sales Considerations

If you plan to retail your fashions over the Internet, getting visitors to your Web site is only half the battle. In order to complete orders online, you will need a shopping cart utility. You do not need to have a system built expressly for your site. There are many services and software packages that will allow your customers to select styles, place orders, and pay on the Internet.

In addition to monthly fees and per transaction charges, some online shopping cart services may take a percentage of the total amount of each purchase. This percentage may decrease at higher sales volumes, so consider your growth predictions and current sales estimates when choosing a plan.

Updates

Creating your Web site should not be a short-term project. If potential customers see old styles and dated information on your Web site, you may lose sales. To maximize the effectiveness of your Web site, keep your inventory, styles, and contact information accurate and up-to-date.

Using an Internet Professional

Even if you hire a Web site designer or programmer to build your Web site, you can save time and money if you can update the site yourself. Make sure you have the files, username, and passwords associated with the site.

There are several simple and inexpensive Web site editors on the market. Being able to manipulate your site yourself will allow you to make small changes and tweaks without paying for a consultant.

Point-of-Sale Systems

A point-of-sale (POS) system can automate inventory management, accounting, and payment processing. POS software and hardware can be a major business expense. Before investing in a POS system, make sure the benefits will outweigh the cost.

Do You Need a POS System?

Whether you sell your garments retail or wholesale, a POS system may help streamline your operations. Your business may be ready for a POS system if:

- You have trouble keeping track of what styles, sizes, and colors are in stock.

- You have a high order fulfillment error rate.

- You seem swamped in paperwork.

- You often run out of materials.

- You have trouble collecting and analyzing sales data.

Common POS System Features

Most POS systems automatically look up the price when a customer buys a garment. The system may update inventory data to reflect deliveries and purchases. Some programs track the company's use of supplies and order materials from suppliers before stores become too low.

POS systems may be integrated with Web sites so that online customers have accurate information about what garments are in stock. Shipping data can be correlated with purchase information so that customers can track their packages. Some POS software stores customer data, which allows the business owner to analyze sales trends.

POS System Requirements

POS systems have different hardware and software requirements. The functionality and power available to you may be limited by your computer's processing speed, memory, and hard drive space.

In addition to a computer to run the POS system and a printer to print out receipts, you will need some way to input data into the system. This could be a keyboard, touch screen, or pointing device. A scanner that reads the barcode from your garment labels can help reduce shipping errors and keep inventory numbers accurate.

Buying a POS System

New POS systems may cost between $2,500 and $6,000. By purchasing new, you often receive training on the system, customization to make sure the system is a good fit with your business, installation, and ongoing technical support. You may also receive free upgrades for a specified length of time.

Used systems start at about $1,500. If you purchase a used system, expect to perform the installation and customization yourself. You may have to pay extra for technical support, if it is available. Some companies do not support outdated systems.

Gathering Information

Most POS systems will store customer purchase, shipping, and billing information and allow you to run reports that sort the information in usable ways. For example, the system may be able to print out a mailing list of customers who bought a particular garment. The list could be used for a direct marketing campaign promoting a coordinating piece.

Processing Credit Card Transactions

Being able to accept credit cards can help improve your bottom line. Retail customers tend to buy more if they can pay by credit card. Boutiques and independent retailers may be more willing to place orders if they have the protection provided by credit card companies.

Credit card companies, banks, and independent sales organizations (ISOs) offer a variety of processing services. Some require businesses to purchase or lease special equipment to read credit cards and transmit the information for verification. Others allow businesses to type the information on a computer and use the Internet to make sure the customer's account is charged appropriately. If you make a high volume of sales at events such as private trunk shows or trade events where there might not be Internet access, you may benefit from a service that lets you process credit card transactions using the telephone.

Credit card processing, or "merchant processing," services may charge you a monthly fee to subscribe to their service in addition to a percentage of each transaction or a flat fee per transaction. You may have a limit to the number of transactions you can process per month without penalty or additional fees.

Information Security

In the course of taking orders and processing payments, you may encounter potentially confidential information about individuals and businesses, such as account numbers and private telephone numbers. If customers suspect that you are not keeping their information secure, they may not trust you with future purchases.

Make sure that the Internet shopping software system you choose uses the highest level of security protocols available. Protect your own computer system from breaches by installing firewalls and checking for viruses regularly.

Some of the most important steps in keeping information safe do not involve computers or technology. Make sure that any unneeded statements are shredded and that you limit the number of people who have access to payment records. If you operate your business from a common area in your home, invest in a lockable file cabinet, and lock it when it is not in use. If you have a separate office or business area, keep it secure. Lost portable devices account for nearly 50 percent of security breaches, so for best security practices, resist the urge to take your laptop or handheld computer out of your office.

Buying Hardware

When purchasing computer hardware, consider the system requirements of your POS, accounting, and design software. Computer-controlled embroidery, knitting, and sewing machines may have specific memory, processing speed, and hard drive size requirements.

Any peripherals you use should be compatible with each other and with your computer system. This includes your printer, credit card and check reader, and bar code scanner.

You can buy computer equipment directly from the manufacturers, from business supply stores, at retail stores, through private sales, and at business auctions. Retail department or electronics stores may offer good deals on hardware geared toward the home office user. These machines will likely be covered by a warranty but may not include customization and technical support.

Computer manufacturers and business supply stores can be the most expensive option, but they usually offer warranty and service packages not available through other markets. In addition, they may have used or refurbished systems that are still under warranty and priced at a discount. When you buy a computer directly from the manufacturer, you may be able to customize the software that comes preinstalled. As a fashion design business owner, you probably will not need the games and personal resources that are standard on many home computers. Being able to purchase only the software you will use may save you substantial money.

Private sales and business auctions are often the least expensive source of computer equipment, but only in rare circumstances will the machines come with a warranty, customization, or technical support.

Buying Software

Fashion design businesses may need a variety of general and specialized applications. Like any other business, you will have to keep track of your finances, manage inventory, communicate with your suppliers and clients, and make decisions. With the right software, your computer can help you with all these tasks.

Bookkeeping software such as QuickBooks or Peachtree can help you manage expense and sales information. If you have employees, these programs can organize records and automate payroll functions. Some programs use the Internet to exchange information with your bank account so you know what electronic payments have arrived and what checks have cleared.

Inventory tracking functions can be part of bookkeeping or POS software, or they may be stand-alone applications. The type of tracking software you need depends on the size and complexity of your line.

Word processing programs are used to write letters and design simple forms. If you plan to design your own marketing materials, you may need publishing software, such as Art Explosion Publisher Pro, Adobe InDesign, or Microsoft Publisher, which will allow you to lay out brochures, postcards, flyers, and catalogs. Most publishing programs come with templates and tutorials to walk you through the design process.

Graphics software such as Adobe Illustrator and Corel Draw can help you create two- and three-dimensional images of your designs. With a few clicks of the mouse, you can see the same look in a different color, shorten a hemline, or add details. If you are screen printing garments, graphics software can create and manipulate images more quickly than working by hand.

If you are designing your own fabric, specialized software such as WeaveIt by The Canyon Art Company will automate draft calculations. Apparel computer aided design (CAD) and computer aided manufacturing (CAM) programs are used to design your garments and lay out the patterns. CAD/CAM programs, such as PolyNest by Polygon Software and Color Matters by Color Matters International Software, allow you to edit and grade your patterns quickly.

Microsoft PowerPoint and Corel Presentations are examples of presentation software. Presentation applications are used to create multimedia presentations that you can use to demonstrate your designs to buyers and introduce your business to potential investors. If you plan to teach workshops or classes in conjunction with your design activities, computerized presentations can help you organize your material and keep your class focused.

If you purchase a computer directly from the manufacturer, you may have the opportunity to buy popular software already installed on your machine. This is called original equipment manufacturer (OEM) software. OEM software that is purchased separately from the hardware it is supposed to accompany will not come with technical support and may not be upgradable. Often, software that is marketed as "OEM" is counterfeit and may cause problems with other software on your computer.

Business programs, such as bookkeeping, appointment management, and word processing software, are also available from business supply stores and software companies. Specialized, industry-specific programs are more likely to be purchased from the software company or through textile equipment dealers. You may be able to purchase this software for a discount when you buy or lease your sewing machine, loom, embroidery machine, or other equipment. Designers who are upgrading their software or closing their business may sell used industry-specific software.

If you purchase used software, whether from a private party or through a dealer, make sure you have all the keys, passwords, and security devices needed to install and use the applications. You may need to pay a fee to the software company to transfer registration of the software. In addition, used software may be several generations old. Before buying preowned software, check to see if the program is still supported by the manufacturer and if it is compatible with your hardware. Once you consider the cost of a license transfer and an upgrade, you may find that it is cheaper and less of a hassle to buy a new version of the software.

If you are a student, you may be able to purchase software at discounted rates. Educational software may have limited functionality, and using it for noneducation purposes probably violates the user licensing agreement. Some companies will allow you to purchase a license upgrade.

Free Software

There are many free or low cost software options for fashion design business owners. **OpenOffice.org** (R) is one of the largest and best supported free productivity suites. It includes a word processor, spreadsheet, presentation editor, graphics editor, and database program. Accounting, inventory management, patternmaking, textile design, and grading patterns are also available for free. **Download.com** is a useful Web site for researching free software.

Unfortunately, free software is often poorly documented or prone to errors. The program might not be updated often enough to remain compatible with other applications or new hardware. If you use free software, do not expect technical support or guarantees against lost or corrupt data.

CASE STUDY: KRISTAN'S CROSSES AND CUSTOM JEWELRY

Kristan Payne, Owner
Kristan's Crosses and Custom Jewelry
www.KristansCross.com
Kristan@KristansCross.com

I started making jewelry when my oldest son wanted to make a cornucopia pattern. At the craft store, we found a pattern for a wire cross. I started playing with the beads and wires and could not stop. After a while, I had hundreds of these crosses, so I started going to craft shows to sell them.

The craft shows did not go over very well. My first year I went to four but only made my entrance fee back on two. I would have stopped, but my boys, Nathaniel, Gabriel, and Caleb, loved them. They learned to price items based on the cost of material and labor and how to make change. Without them, I would still be playing with wire and beads.

People at craft shows started to ask about jewelry, so I started making necklaces and earrings. My jewelry began to sell so I continued doing shows. My son Gabriel started his own line of earrings called Gabe's Jewelry.

The boys and I have so much fun at shows. We love meeting people that we otherwise would not. Craft show sales can be very volatile. When the economy is bad, people are afraid to spend too much money.

I started my Web site mainly as a form of publicity. To sell on the Internet, you have to be found by your customers. EBay is a hard place for jewelers to sell because there is so much going for so cheap.

In the future, I hope to improve my Web site so that I can take orders, to do more custom orders, and to start hosting home parties where people can make their own jewelry.

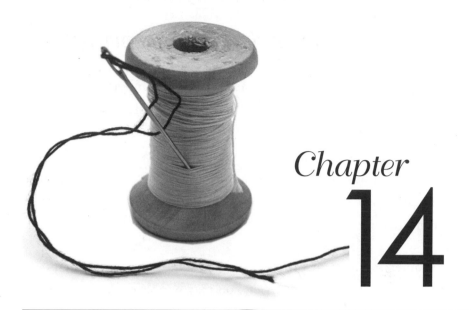

Keeping Your Customers Happy

Whether your customers are corporate buyers or retail consumers, when they are pleased with their purchase, they will be more likely to buy more garments from you in the future.

Defining Customer Service

Customer service includes any procedure that affects a customer's purchasing experience. Making it easy and pleasant to view your line, order garments, receive shipments, and make returns is as important to customer service as the quality of your clothing. Customer service includes how you interact with your customers, including how you react to special requests and handle problems.

Why is Customer Service Important?

The customer service you provide is one of your most important marketing tools. Members of your target market are likely to share their purchasing experiences, whether they were good or bad, with each other. A reputation for poor customer service can reduce your sales. Wholesale and retail buyers have plenty of fashion lines to choose from. They do not want to have to deal with someone who will not bend on shipping terms or help solve sizing concerns.

The customer service you provide can help your line stand out in the fashion industry. As a small business, you may be able to be more flexible than the larger, more established companies. If a buyer has a problem with a garment or a special request for alterations or packaging, you are able to deal with the customer directly and find a solution. In larger companies, the customer may have to deal with multiple management layers.

This flexibility can be a powerful branding strategy, but it can also lead to cash flow problems. Corporate buyers in particular may try to push you to compromise on contract terms past the point of good customer service. Keep a close eye on your profit margin to make sure that any concessions you make do not hit your bottom line too hard.

Good customer service goes beyond making sure people who purchase your designs are satisfied. Everyone who attends a trunk show, visits your retail space, or attends one of your workshops is a potential customer. Just because they do not buy a garment that day does not mean they never will. If you treat them with the same courtesy you show the people who are buying your clothes, "just lookers" may become buyers in the future.

Who is Responsible for Customer Service?

Everyone in your operation can help improve the purchasing experience, but good customer service has to begin at the top. As the owner of a fashion design business, you are responsible for making customer service a top priority. If you act as if a client is unimportant, that attitude will influence your staff.

Some ways to set a tone of good customer service throughout your business include:

- Treat your employees with respect. Address problems privately.

- Train your staff in the importance of good customer service.

- Give employees the authority to handle customer service issues.

- Make sure sale representatives know about the features and benefits of your designs.

- Think about how you will handle returned shipments, canceled orders, and customer complaints before they happen.

- Model good customer service practices. Do not do anything you would not want a staff member doing.

Addressing Customer Concerns

Some customer service concerns are specific to the fashion industry. Being aware of these issues can help you establish procedures to try to prevent them. Because of human error, manufacturing issues, and material flaws, mistakes will likely happen. Having written plans to deal with common problems can help you provide good customer service.

Sizing

Garment sizing can be confusing to designers, consumers, and retailers — especially in women's fashions where there is no standard size scale. Most retail stores prefer consistent sizing between the lines they carry. Shoppers may expect to try on two or three different sizes to get a good fit, but they may become frustrated and confused if sizes vary too much.

Fashion designers who sell to more than one retail store may find it hard to match the size standards of each. What is sold as a size 8 in one store may be a size 2 in another. One way to match several different scales is to label your garments with waist, chest, and length dimensions rather than numerical sizes. As you fill orders to retailers, you can sew in additional labels with sizes that correspond to your buyers' requirements.

If you retail your own designs, consider offering to exchange garments or refund the purchase price when customers return clothing because of sizing problems. Displaying actual garment measurements can help minimize size confusion on Internet or catalog purchases. A high rate of size-related complaints about a particular style may indicate mislabeling or a grading error.

Fit

Some garments have disproportionate measurements that cause fit rather than sizing issues. For example, a customer may return a pair of jeans that fits in the waist and inseam but is too wide in the hips. Most fit complaints can be resolved by refunding the purchase price on receipt of the garment.

Complaints about poor fit may stem from differences in people's bodies, the design of the garment, or grading errors. Some designers differentiate their lines by catering to fit preferences and cutting their garments with long waists, short inseams, wide chests, or other silhouette adjustments.

If the garment has fit flaws because of mistakes in the pattern or manufacturing errors, track down the source of the problem and correct it in future runs of the garment. If you sell your products wholesale, the retailers will likely know about the problem before you do, as they are the people dealing with the complaining customers. Work with your retailers to find a resolution to the situation. Some stores may prefer to pull the flawed garments from the sales floor and send them back to you. Others may agree to attempt to sell the garments at reduced prices to recover some of the manufacturing costs.

If the cutting and sewing directions were not followed when the garments were produced, the manufacturer may be liable for part or all the losses from the flawed pieces.

Care Labeling

The instructions you provide for washing, drying, and ironing your designs should minimize the chance of damage, fading, color bleeding, and shrinkage. Make sure you test your instructions on the finished garment, not just the components. Component pieces of different fibers or weaves may react to temperature or agitation differently. For example, if the trim of a skirt shrinks more than the body, washing and drying the garment according to the care instructions may cause unattractive puckering.

In addition to testing the recommended care instructions, experimenting with other common care procedures may help you develop more complete care instructions. For example, if you discover that using steam on a knit acrylic sweater makes it lose elasticity, you can include an appropriate warning on the care label.

Packaging

Customers may complain if a garment arrives wrinkled, stretched, or damaged because of the packaging. A silk shirt shipped loose in a box is likely to become unfolded, wrinkled, and unattractive before it reaches its destination. Fragile beads or buttons may be crushed unless they have protective wrapping. You may handle complaints about poorly packaged items by offering to replace the damaged goods or to refund the purchase price.

Planning and experience can help reduce packaging-related complaints. Avoid boxes that are significantly larger than required. Fold lightweight garments around cardstock or cardboard, and use pins or tape to help the fabric keep shape. Reinforce collars with shapers. Tape foam around trim that may get crushed during shipping. Wrap folded garments in plastic to protect them from objectionable odors.

Stores may refuse shipments that are not packaged according to the purchasing agreement, so review wholesale contracts carefully before sending the order. If you do not think the packaging directions provided by the buyer are enough to protect the garments, discuss alternatives with your client. Consider insuring your shipment so that you will be protected if the package is damaged or lost.

Label Placement

Customers may complain if the care instructions, fiber content, manufacturing identification, and country of origin labels are hard to find or uncomfortable. Avoid layering tags, which can cause stiff seams, bulges, and pressure points. Tags placed where they are likely to rub the wearer's skin, such as at the back of the neck or waistband, should be soft and flexible.

Required information can be printed directly to the inside of the garment so that there are no tags. Federal guidelines require that tagless labels, like traditional sewn labels, remain legible and attached for the life of the garment.

Workmanship

Depending on the complexity of a style, there may be many places where manufacturing errors can occur. For example, a skirt hem might hang awkwardly, a pants zipper might not stay up, or a seam might be missing stitches. In many cases, garments returned because of workmanship-related concerns may be repaired and returned to the retail floor.

If you notice a trend of customer complaints or returns because of workmanship issues, try to pinpoint the source of the errors so that they can be prevented in the future. If you find that trimmings or fasteners are at fault, contact your supplier so that it knows there is a problem. If the problem is with the manufacturing process, discuss it with your contractor.

At low quantities, it may be practical to examine every garment before it is sent to the retail or wholesale customer. At higher quantities, sample garments can be inspected at key points in the design process. By checking a percentage of each style when it arrives from the factory, when it is sent to customers, and when it arrives at the retailer, workmanship-related problems may be reduced.

Color

Customers may be dissatisfied with a garment if the color is not what they expected. This is a primarily a problem for Internet or catalog sales where monitors and printer ink may not reproduce colors accurately. However, color-related problems can also occur with in-store purchases if lighting or background designs interfere with how the customer perceives the color.

In addition to showing pictures of each garment and color choice in your print or online catalog, consider adding descriptions of the hues. Avoid vague phrases like "heavenly blue" or "feisty red." Instead, try to stick with standard modifiers that your customers are likely to recognize, such as "royal blue" or "candy apple red."

If the color of a garment does not match a widely recognizable term, try to describe the color as accurately and simply as possible. A yellow blouse may appear off-white on some computers and orange on others. Describing it as "medium yellow with just a touch of green" can help reduce confusion.

Swatches can be helpful to customers who need to find a particular color. You can package swatches individually or in books containing all the fabrics used in a collection. Consider including swatches in your catalog or sales kit to help minimize color-related returns.

Material Flaws

Color, texture, and printing inconsistencies on fabric or trim may be the result of improper handling or flawed material. If you notice stains, rips, holes, or fading on a garment, review your procedures to try to pinpoint the cause of the damage. For example, if you often have food or beverages nearby while you are folding or inspecting garments, a drop may have gotten on the fabric. Sunlight from the window in the storage room may have caused fading.

Complaints about material flaws can be minimized by thoroughly inspecting all fabric, fasteners, decorations, and trimmings that you purchase. The quality assurance practices used to detect workmanship errors can also help identify material flaws before faulty garments are available to consumers.

Shipping

Customers may complain about slow or overpriced shipping. To help reduce shipping-related issues, offer customers several choices in delivery time and cost. Most carriers now have cost estimators available through their Web sites. Keep a postal scale and a selection of standard-sized boxes on hand so you can give customers an accurate delivery estimate. Unless an order requires special packaging, do not add exorbitant handling charges.

Customer Service Decisions

An important step in defining customer service policies is developing a customer service philosophy for your business. Although you may decide to make satisfying your customers a high priority, in order to build a financially successful business you will have to balance the concessions you give to customers with the profit margin of the transaction. Although it may be better in the long run to take an occasional loss in the name of customer service, continuously giving in to retail or wholesale buyers may jeopardize your operation.

Thinking about the ethical issues of customer service can help you decide how far you will go to please your clientele.

Selling Dangerous Products

If a customer complains about a potential health or safety issue, you will have to decide whether to pull all the garments of that style or let them remain on the sales floor. If you knowingly let a dangerous product be sold, you may be held liable in the event of injury, illness, or death related to that product.

Selling Garments with Known Flaws

If you realize that a design was manufactured with a cutting or construction flaw, you have several options. You can continue to sell the garments without mentioning the flaw to your customer. Alternatively, you can reveal the flaw and offer the garments at reduced prices. Another choice is to destroy the garments or sell them to closeout retailers.

If you decide to sell a flawed garment, you risk damaging your label's image. Even if an unsatisfied customer does not take the time to return a purchase, he or she is less likely to buy one of your designs again. One way to combat this is to remove labels that refer to your company. If you go this route, make sure your garments still meet the Federal Trade Commission labeling requirements.

Selling Garments with Potential Flaws

After receiving your completed garments, you may find that a percentage of your inventory has a flaw. Perhaps some zippers are faulty or the adhesive on the decorations fails if not applied correctly.

As a business owner, you will have to weigh the financial loss of recalling or wasting the potentially flawed inventory against the image and customer satisfaction risks of leaving the inventory on the market. The decision you make may depend on the cost of replacing the merchandise, the severity of the flaw, and the percent of garments likely to be affected.

Selling Returned Garments

No matter how tight your quality assurance procedures, odds are you will have merchandise returned at some point. Some fashion businesses send all returned merchandise to the clearance rack or to closeout retailers. Others return garments to the retail floor or to inventory for future order fulfillment.

A third option is to resell garments that are returned for customer-related reasons, while sending those returned for garment-related reasons to the secondary market. Under this policy, if a shirt is returned because the customer needs a different size or decided he does not like the color, the shirt could be returned to the sale inventory. However, if the shirt was returned because of a small stain on the collar, the shirt would be set aside for the off-sale market.

Exchanging Garments

If a wholesale, catalog, or Internet customer wishes to exchange a garment for one of another size, style, or color, there may be shipping costs involved with returning the unwanted merchandise and sending the replacement.

Wholesale contracts may spell out who pays shipping under different situations. In the case of retail customers, having written return and exchange policies can help minimize disputes about shipping payment. If a customer is returning a garment because of a manufacturing error or material flaw, paying the postage both ways can help increase their satisfaction with the transaction.

Refunds

In some cases, a customer may prefer a refund to a merchandise exchange.

Your refund policy should address the condition merchandise must be in to qualify for a refund and the window of time after purchase during which a refund will be available. It is common to require the customer to present a receipt in order to issue a refund.

Refunds can be issued as a credit card chargeback, a check written to the customer, or cash. It is common to use the same method as the customer used when paying for the merchandise. If a customer paid by check, confirm with your bank that the check has cleared before issuing a refund.

Store Credit

You may decide to issue store credit instead of a refund if a customer does not have a receipt for the returned merchandise. Store credit can be issued in the form of a store debit card, a gift certificate, a note in your accounting software, or an edited receipt. When issuing store credit, make sure you note the amount, date, and customer's name in your bookkeeping records.

Developing Customer Service Policies

After you have decided the approaches you will take to solve common customer service issues, take the time to put your policy in writing and make it available to your customers and employees.

A written customer service policy can serve as a guide for handling situations, which will allow employees to take care of them on their own. When your customers do not have to wait for you to process their returns or manage their complaints, you, your employees, and your customers are likely to be less frustrated.

A written customer service policy may also provide some legal protection.

If a boutique owner demands a full refund on garments she purchased six months ago but was unable to sell, the terms of your contract or sales agreement will determine what type and amount of refund, if any, you are required to give. For this reason, it is a good idea to include a copy of your customer service policy in your sales agreements.

Writing a Customer Service Policy

A customer service policy should address specific actions that will be taken in response to common situations. The policy should lay out the responsibilities of the customer as well as those of the business.

Some issues to address in the customer service policy include ordering, payment, shipping, returns, and customer privacy. Make sure to include details. Your policy should try to reduce customer confusion and frustration.

Ordering

In your customer service policy, list all of the ways customers can order your products. Include contact information for each ordering method. If you accept telephone orders, include your telephone number. If you accept faxed orders, list your fax number and add a sample order form. If you send out catalogs or sales kits, tell potential customers how to get on your mailing list.

Payment

List the different ways customers can pay for their orders. If different sales terms apply for certain methods, be sure to include the details. For example, you may choose not to ship orders that have been paid for by check until the check clears. List the different types of credit cards you can process in addition to any online payment services you accept. If you will allow wholesale customers to buy on credit, list the qualification and payment terms.

If you plan on accepting checks, detail the amount you will charge if the check is returned because of a closed account or insufficient funds.

Shipping

In addition to listing the different carriers and delivery options from which your customers can choose, include the approximate time it will take you to fill orders.

Returns

Your written return policy should include how long a customer has to return a garment and the paperwork that should accompany any returns. List how much and what type of compensation customers will receive for items returned for different reasons and in different condition. Detail what types of returns qualify for full or partial refunds and which are eligible only for exchanges. List if refunds will be issued as cash, check, or store credit. Describe who is responsible for shipping costs under different circumstances.

In your written policy, include the procedures customers should follow to initiate a return. Do they need to contact you first to get a return merchandise authorization (RMA) number? Give the address where they should send the merchandise and any forms that need to be completed. Provide estimates regarding how long customers will have to wait for their refunds and your contact information for further information.

Customer Privacy

A privacy statement can be part of your customer service policy or a separate document. In the course of marketing your garments, processing and fulfilling orders, and accepting payments, you are likely to gather large amounts of information about your customers. Some customers worry about who will have access to their credit card account number, or if their home or e-mail address will be sold to marketers.

Internet privacy is another potential issue for some customers. In addition to reporting on visitor activity on your Web site, some monitoring software will track visitor behavior after they leave your site, including other Web sites visited, online purchases, and search engine queries. Some customers may view this level of monitoring as invasive. If you are using monitoring software to learn about your target market, you should reveal in your privacy statement what information is gathered.

Your privacy statement should also address who will be able to view customer records and whether any information you gather will be sold. You should disclose if you plan on sending promotional or marketing material to the customer's e-mail or mailing address. Some jurisdictions require that customers "opt in to," or expressly agree to receive, promotional mailings. At the least, you should provide your customers with an easy way to "opt out of," or remove their contact information from, mailing lists.

Publishing Your Policy

Your customer service policy should be phrased as simply as possible. The information should be laid out clearly and in a way that helps the reader find the information he or she needs quickly and easily.

If you have different policies and procedures for different types of customers, you may need several versions of your customer service policy. For example, your return terms may be different for wholesale customers than for retail customers. Listing both policies in one document may be confusing.

In addition, you may find it helpful to have an internal version of the policy with procedures to help employees handle product returns, sales inquiries, and customer complaints.

Because of the importance of the document, a lawyer should review your customer service policies to make sure the terms are legal and worded appropriately.

Distributing Your Policy

After you have completed your customer service policy, you need to make it available to your target market. If you have a business Web site, consider including a prominent link to a copy of your policy. If you sell most of your garments through personal contact, include your policy in the purchase agreement, or print it on the back of the customer's order form copy. You may also want to print a copy on your receipts and add a copy to shipping invoices.

If you have a retail space, consider displaying a sign that lists important parts of your policy, including returned check fees and merchandise return procedures.

Making Exceptions

There may be times when you decide to make exceptions to your written policy. Giving repeat or high-volume buyers special terms may encourage future purchases. Making concessions to customers with special needs or in emergency situations can foster customer loyalty.

Wholesale buyers may have their own standard purchasing contracts. If their preferred terms are significantly different than yours, you may need to compromise your policies in order to close the sale.

Policy Updates

There are several reasons you may need to update your customer service policy. You may find that some of your procedures are no longer needed. For example, if you contract with a check verification service, you may no longer need a returned check policy. If you stop the retail side of your operation, you can remove any instructions for retail returns and exchanges.

You may find that some parts of your policy discourage potential customers from purchasing your garments. If you do not accept returned merchandise for any reason, customers may feel that buying from you is too risky. If you charge an excessive price for shipping and handling, customers may feel that they are being taken advantage of.

If you decide to edit your policy, make sure that the all online and in print copies of the policy are revised.

Customer Incentive Programs

Today's customers have choices in where to buy their fashions. Your target market may be overwhelmed with opportunities to spend money. Whether you cater to retail or wholesale buyers, incentive programs can help convince customers to try your garments, place large orders, and make repeat purchases.

The incentives you offer should be tailored to the behavior you want to encourage in your potential customers. If you want to entice new buyers, consider offering a free garment or accessory on first-time purchases. Free shipping on orders over a certain amount can increase customer spending. Free merchandise or store credit after a specified purchase volume can keep customers coming back to you. Free or low cost alterations and special sales events can also help encourage future purchases.

Incentive programs are not limited to retail customers. You can also develop programs to encourage store owners and corporate buyers to give your line a try or to place bigger or more frequent orders. No-hassle exchange policies, free merchandise, and frequent buyer rewards can be as effective on wholesale buyers as they are on retail consumers. In order to avoid the stigma of offering shady kickbacks, make sure any incentive programs you have are fully documented in your sales kit. Be aware that some businesses will not allow employees to accept gifts from suppliers.

You may find it profitable to target incentive programs toward the people who will be selling your garments directly to the retail customers. These may be your employees or the salespeople at the stores that carry your designs. You may decide to offer a gift or store credit to anyone who sells a certain amount of your merchandise during a specified week or month. Alternatively, you might have one prize for the salesperson in each store who sells the most from your line.

Special Concerns for Custom Designers

Businesses that sell custom, one of a kind, or "wearable art" garments have some additional customer service considerations. Designers for these companies often work directly with their clients to create unique clothing. When something goes wrong with an order, customers do not simply return the garment to the retailer — they blame the designer.

Because custom designers tend to have a closer relationship with their clients than other fashion designers, providing stellar customer service is crucial. Not every custom project will turn out as planned, but handling problems politely and professionally can help increase customer satisfaction and loyalty.

Communicating with Clients

Customer service issues related to custom designs may be prevented simply by talking with your clients. Keep a file for each project you work on. Include notes of every conversation you have with the client. Document the time and date of the conversation, what you talked about, and any decisions that were made. This will help protect you in case of a misunderstanding and save you from having to remember every fabric, style, and payment detail. Keep a copy of the work order or project agreement in the project file, along with any notes you have about the design. If you will be contracting out any of the work or purchasing new materials, file the receipts.

Whether you communicate with your client through a formal, in-person interview, a casual telephone chat, or a series of e-mails, ask questions until you know exactly what your customer wants. The golden rule of custom design is not to leave anything to chance.

Some points you may want to clarify with your client include:

- **Is the outfit for a special event?** If so, make sure you will be able to get the finished garment to the customer well before the event's date. Clarify how formal the event will be and the expected weather.

- **How many times does the client intend to wear the garment?** Clothing that will be worn and laundered multiple times may need different construction considerations than a garment that will be worn only once and then packed away.

- **How does the client intend to care for the garment?** If the customer does not like to hand wash or dry clean clothes, your fabric and construction choices will be limited.

- **Does the client have any special needs?** If the garment will be used for a performance or sporting event, you may need to use technical fabrics and sturdier construction. If the client has a limited range of motion, you may need to size and place fasteners and openings carefully.

- **What image does the client want to project** while wearing the garment? Does he want to look sexy, professional, casual, or mature?

- **What body or facial features does the client love?** What does she want to hide? The cut and design features you choose can draw the viewer's eye to or away from certain areas.

Time Issues

For custom fashion businesses, meeting deadlines is a constant challenge. Machines tend to break down, staff members get sick, and materials become delayed at the worst possible times. Even if you have a reasonable explanation for failing to complete a garment on time, a customer will know only that his order is late.

Once you realize that you are not going to meet a deadline, you have several options for handling the situation. You can sacrifice the quality of the garment by taking design or construction shortcuts in order to make up for lost time. Although this strategy can help you meet the deadline, your customer may still end up disappointed if the final product does not meet expectations.

Another option is to be up-front with your client about the status of the project. If she is not planning on wearing the garment for an upcoming event, she may not mind granting a deadline extension. If time is critical, the client might have some preferences of what can be cut or changed to help finish the garment quickly. For example, you may be able to redesign a formal gown to need less beading or to have a less intricate hem line.

When preparing an estimate for a custom order, consider adding extra time to allow for mistakes and unforeseen events that can put you behind schedule. Few clients will complain if an order is finished early.

Delivery Issues

Because custom items can be difficult or impossible to replace, take extra care when packing and shipping orders. Make sure that fragile parts of a garment, such as buttons or glass beading, are protected with appropriate wrapping and cushions.

In addition, consider purchasing insurance with your shipping service. Insurance covers merchandise that is lost, stolen, or damaged in transit. The shipping company may not retain records of insurance purchases, so make sure to file the receipt of any packages you insure.

Quality Issues

Thanks to the Internet and the global economy, ordering a custom garment does not mean visiting your local tailor or dressmaker and attending multiple fittings. Some clients are separated from their designer by great distances and never get to touch or try on their custom pieces until the work is completed and the bill is paid.

Once they see the finished products, customers may not be completely happy with the results. The color might not be what they expected, the fabric might not be as soft or heavy as they hoped, or the craftsmanship may not be as exquisite as they were led to believe.

If a customer complains to you about the quality of an order, take all comments seriously. If you take the position that all sales are final, you may lose repeat business and find your reputation declining among your target market. Instead, talk with your client and try to find the heart of the problem. If the fit is uncomfortable or incorrect, offer to alter the garment. If the color is wrong, determine if you can safely dye the garment. Decorations, fasteners, seams, and hems can sometimes be altered without much trouble.

If your client is disappointed with the craftsmanship of the piece, find out all the details you can about where the construction fell short of expectations. Fix the garment if possible. If not, consider offering a full refund on the return of the garment.

Remember to stay calm and not to take the criticism personally.

The best way to prevent quality issues is to describe your designs accurately. Avoid exaggerating the material, style, or workmanship. Correct any errors you find before the garment leaves your workshop. Fix even tiny flaws. Be a perfectionist when it comes to your clothes. It is your reputation that is on the line.

Fixing mistakes may require additional material, trim, fasteners, or decorations. Custom fashion design businesses can lose money if they purchase extra supplies. On the other hand, if the seamstress makes a mistake when cutting the material or there is a flaw in a decoration, the lost time and extra expense of shipping in replacement supplies may cost even more money.

Manufacturing Issues

Fabric mills routinely introduce new styles and discontinue outdated or low-selling material. This means that the silk organza your client fell in love with in your sample book may not be available when she is ready to order.

Customers usually understand if the fabric or trim they chose was discontinued. Although they may be disappointed, they may be willing to work with you to find a suitable alternative. Consult your client before making a substitution. Even if you are certain he or she will not notice the change, you may be in violation of your contract if you do not use the exact materials agreed on.

Meeting Clients' Expectations

When clients do not understand fashion's specialized terminology, it can be difficult for them to communicate their vision with the designer. Even if the designer does create the exact look the customer had in mind, the client might have second thoughts after trying the garment on.

If your customer is disappointed with the custom order but is not able to point to a specific fit, style, material, or craftsmanship issue, you may find it impossible to fix the problem. Talk to your client and try to pinpoint what was expected and where the finished garment fell short. Some questions to consider that might help you both understand the situation include:

- How does the customer feel when she puts on the garment? How did she hope to feel?

- What one thing would the customer change about the garment?

- What catches the customer's attention when she sees herself in the mirror wearing the garment?

- What does the customer want people to think when they see her wearing the garment?

If you suspect that some of your client's requests will detract from the outfit, speak up. Offer alternatives. You are the expert. If you have concerns, discuss them with your client. You might discover that you do not quite understand the customer's vision. To help avoid misunderstandings and dashed hopes, sketch your designs as they would appear on the client's body. Save the disproportionate fashion drawings for sales agents and magazine editors.

Sometimes clients have unrealistic expectations for their custom garment. They may hope that the clothes make them look significantly thinner, younger, or sexier. There is not much you can do if this is the case. Consider offering a full refund if the customer wants to return the garment. Look over your project notes and see if you can see any ways you could have prevented the situation.

The Hard-to-Please Customer

You may occasionally find a client who is not satisfied with the size, color, price, or cut of a garment or a wholesale buyer who wants to negotiate every point in the sales contract. Keep the following pointers in mind when dealing with a difficult customer:

- **Stay calm**. You are more likely to work out a solution if the encounter does not turn into a screaming match.

- ❦ **Act professionally**. Resist the urge to vent to your employees or other customers.

- ❦ **Breaking your policies** can be a solution, but it can cause new problems. Some customers may be placated by special treatment. Others, however, may push even harder to get additional concessions.

- ❦ **Try not to take complaints personally**. Although it can be hard to separate yourself from something you designed or created, it can be easier to deal with a problem if you do not consider it an insult on your talent or abilities.

- ❦ **Take a time-out**. If you are getting too upset by a situation, take a few minutes to yourself before returning a call or e-mail from a disgruntled customer.

Although most customers are willing to work with designers to fix problems, there are always a few who can always find something else to complain about. You will have to decide when it is in the best financial interest of your business to stop trying to please a difficult customer.

CASE STUDY: KELLY BANNISTER

Kelly Bannister, Synchronized Swimming and Dance Competition Costume Designer

I started designing costumes when my children were involved in synchronized swimming. The first competition their team went to, our girls were very underclothed. It was hard to find nice costumes, and the ones we could find were very expensive, ranging from $800 to $900 per costume.

Another mother and I bought some swimsuits in bulk and added beadwork

CASE STUDY: KELLY BANNISTER

and sequins. It took about a week for each costume. We created headpieces and tiaras. Later, we made flashier costumes with rhinestones for larger competitions. Some of our designs were even seen in national swimming competitions.

I found that the skills I learned designing swimwear could also be used to create custom dance competition costumes. Dancewear is a challenge because you need certain details to be visible from a distance. For example, I once created a scarecrow costume that was filled with sequins and rhinestones so that it would shine from the stage.

One thing I learned was that you have to use high-quality materials. Cheap crystals and beading may look all right in your hand, but from a distance they will not perform well.

Costume designers need to adapt quickly. You may need to go with your clients to important competitions and make changes on the spot. A hot glue gun is a necessity. No one cares how the costume is put together, as long as it looks good on stage.

My advice for new costume designers is to learn about stage effects. Worry about how your design will look at a distance and under lights, not about the little details no one will see.

Chapter

15

Staff Issues

W hen you start your fashion design business your staff is likely to consist of you and, if you are lucky, one or two close friends willing to work in exchange for free clothes and coffee. As your business grows, however, you may find that you need to hire seasonal, part-time, or full-time employees to keep up with the demand.

Employee Roles

There are many possible job titles within the fashion design business. The employees you choose to hire depend on what role you wish to have in your business.

If you operate a retail space in addition to design work, you may eventually need to hire a retail manager. A retail manager organizes store operations, sets in-store customer service policies, displays merchandise, develops store promotions, and helps set prices. In addition, the retail manager hires, trains, and schedules store employees.

If you sell to stores across the country, a sales representative plans sales trips, meets with and shows your lines to buyers, negotiates contracts, and writes orders. Sales representatives may be paid based on the amount of merchandise they sell.

If you produce a large quantity of garments, a purchasing agent can help save you time and money. A purchasing agent researches vendors and finds the best prices on fabric, findings, trim, and fasteners that meet the designer's and manufacturer's needs.

A sourcing agent has the same function as a purchasing agent but focuses on finding production sites for your designs. In addition to researching manufacturers and negotiating contract terms, a sourcing agent inspects facilities to make sure labor laws are enforced.

Quality assurance managers work with production facilities to minimize quality issues on your garments. If a problem is found, the quality assurance manager looks for the cause and develops a correction plan. The quality assurance manager writes procedures for inspecting garments throughout the manufacturing process.

As your business grows, you may need to hire another designer or an assistant designer to help create fashions for your label. Assistant designers usually help and interpret design sketches by working with patternmakers and fit models. Designers develop the concept of garments and lines.

If you receive regular online, catalog, or wholesale sales, you may need employees to fill and ship orders. In addition, you may find it more convenient and cost effective to hire patternmakers and production staff rather than contract the work out.

Full-Time, Part-Time, Contract, and Seasonal Employees

Most roles in a fashion design business can be filled by full-time, part-time, contract, or seasonal employees. The choice for each job depends on the amount of work that needs to be completed and the time commitment you will require from the staff members.

Full-time employees usually work at least 35 hours per week and are paid a salary. They usually receive benefits such as health insurance and paid vacations. Part-time employees usually work less than 35 hours per week and are paid by the hour. Some businesses provide benefits for part-time employees. Contract employees may be paid by the job or receive a commission for their work. Seasonal employees are hired for only a short time and may be paid by the hour. Contract and seasonal employees usually do not receive benefits.

In the fashion industry, highly qualified professionals are often available for part-time, contract, or seasonal employment. Designers may be looking for paying projects to help finance their own lines. Purchasing and sourcing agents might work part time for several businesses. Some sales representatives specialize in specific target markets and sell accessories, sportswear, lingerie, and outerwear from several lines.

Management Duties

Once you hire your first employee, you become a personnel manager. In addition to your regular business activities, you now have the responsibility to define duties, provide feedback, train your staff, and follow labor laws. Qualified employees can help take some of the burden of running a business off your shoulders, but they also add another layer of complexity to accounting, taxing, and long-term planning.

Developing Employee Policies

Staff members and managers are more comfortable and secure if expectations and goals are clearly defined. Make sure each employee has a clear understanding of his or her job description, duties, and compensation structure. Depending on the roles your employees play in your fashion design business, other procedures may also need defining.

Compensation

Determine which jobs will be filled by salaried employees, hourly employees, and contract workers. Set standard hourly and per job rates that are fair to your employees and allow a satisfactory profit margin. Sales representatives may be paid a commission that ranges between 10 and 15 percent of the sales they bring in. Decide how often you will pay your employees and if sales representatives will receive their commission when orders are placed, when customers pay, or when merchandise is delivered.

Supplies and Tools

Will you provide supplies to employees, or are they expected to provide their own? Make sure all employees understand who is responsible for purchasing sketch pads, paints, and pattern paper. If you hire contractors to sew your samples or inventory, discuss whether they will be working on your machines or their own.

Travel Expenses

How will you reimburse sales representatives who have to travel to meet with potential customers and sourcing agents who need to inspect factories? Will you pay for their expenses or set a per day allowance? Will there be a limit to the type of restaurant, hotel, or airline ticket they will be reimbursed for?

Training and Education

Employees may take classes, conferences, or workshops that increase their value to your company. Will you reimburse them for part or all the costs?

Overtime

Federal and state laws determine how much you are required to pay hourly employees who work more than 40 hours a week, but how will you reimburse salaried or contract employees who put in extra hours to finish a project or prepare for an event? Make sure your employees are informed if you do not intend to pay additional compensation.

Revisions

How many revisions will you expect contract designers, fashion artists, or craftspeople to complete? Are you willing to pay extra for corrections?

Use of Company Resources

Are employees allowed to work on their own designs during company time or sew their own clothing using your sewing machines? Do they need to provide their own supplies?

Creative Ownership

Who owns the ideas and designs your employees develop? Will employees be able to use the techniques you teach them outside the business or reproduce your designs for personal or professional use?

Competitors

Will you limit their ability to design for your current customers or target market while they work with you or after they leave your employment?

Outside Incentives

Purchasing and sourcing agents are sometimes offered gifts from vendors and manufacturers. Are your employees allowed to accept these gifts? How should they document them? Are they allowed to let outside incentives influence their business decisions?

The Employee Handbook

Writing down your policies and distributing them to your staff can help clarify employment issues and protect you in case there is a misunderstanding about procedures or reimbursement.

The employee handbook should cover job duties, pay structure, benefits, travel reimbursement, customer service policies, noncompete agreements, scheduling, and evaluation procedures. It is a good idea to have a lawyer review your employee handbook to make sure your policies meet federal and local regulations. Have copies of your employee handbook printed and bound. Issue a handbook to each employee and keep copies at your office and retail site.

The Federal Labor Standards Act requires that employers define job expectations and communicate them clearly to their staff members. In order to document that you have met this requirement, make sure each employee signs a statement that he or she received and read an employee handbook, and keep the signed records in the appropriate employee files.

Hiring Staff Members

Hiring an employee with a good work ethic and the skills you require can be challenging. Searching for applicants in the right places, carefully screening candidates, and giving your staff appropriate training can minimize the frustration.

Advertising for Employees

Newspaper advertisements can be appropriate when looking for retail sales or order fulfillment staff. If you live in a large city, they may also be used to find designers, sales representatives, and purchasing agents. Fashion professionals can also be found through ads in industry publications or by networking at events.

Some Web sites specialize in matching contract workers with employers. Local employment agencies may provide you with seasonal help.

You may choose to collect résumés or to have candidates complete an application form. If you use an application form, make sure that it includes a place for the applicant's contact information, the job for which he or she is applying, and a summary of education and work experience. You may also want to ask for references.

The following sample application form is also found on the accompanying CD.

JOB APPLICATION FORM	
Applicant's last name	
First name	
Middle name	
Nickname	
Social Security Number	
Street address	
City	
State	
Zip code	
Phone number	
Are you eligible to work in the United States?	
Have you been convicted or pled no contest to a felony within the last seven years? If yes, please explain:	
Position applied for:	
Hours available:	
Monday:	
Tuesday:	
Wednesday:	
Thursday:	
Friday:	

JOB APPLICATION FORM	
Saturday:	
Sunday:	
Summary of education:	
Summary of employment (please attach résumé if available):	
Reference name:	
Reference address:	
Reference telephone:	
Reference name:	
Reference address:	
Reference telephone:	
May we contact your references?	
I certify that the information above is complete and true. I understand that providing false information on this application may be grounds for not hiring me or for immediate dismissal.	
Signature:	
Date:	

Interviewing Applicants

The goal of advertising for employees is to find a selection of qualified candidates in the hope that one of them will have the personality and availability to work well with your organization.

It may be preferable to interview potential employees rather than choosing one based on a portfolio or résumé. By talking with candidates, you will get a chance to ask specific questions about their work philosophy and experiences. An interview will also give applicants a chance to clarify their understanding of the job descriptions and compensation.

Job interviews can be as stressful for business owners as they are for applicants. Be on time, prepared, and courteous for an interview. Highly qualified professionals are likely to have a choice of employers. When you find the perfect candidate for a position, you will want that person to like your business and be excited about working for you.

Hold interviews in a private setting with minimal disruptions. Have the details of the position, including the job descriptions, duties, pay, benefits, and work schedule available.

Have a list of questions ready, but try to keep the interview as relaxed and conversational as possible. Some possible questions include what the applicants expect from a manager, how well they work in teams, when they are available to start working, and what they see themselves doing in ten years.

Some topics are not appropriate for job interviews. Federal law prohibits questions about the job candidate's race, religion, ethnicity, sexuality, health, nationality, or gender. Your questions should not deal with these subjects either directly or indirectly. Avoid any personal questions and focus on the applicant's ability to do the job.

Questions that you should avoid include:

- What part of town did you grow up in? A question like this may be an indirect way of addressing someone's race or national origin.

- Have you had that cough long? Questions about an applicant's health are incompliant with the Americans with Disabilities Act.

- How will your girlfriend feel about you working with models? Do not ask questions about the interviewee's personal relationships or sexuality.

During the interviews, look for an applicant that has the skills required to help your business grow. In addition to technical abilities such as drawing, designing, or sewing, your employee may need communication skills and the capability to work with a team. If you are hiring a retail manager or a designer, you may need someone with leadership skills. If your employee will be handling money or have access to your designs, you will want someone who is trustworthy and honest. Customer service can lead to stressful situations, so anyone in a retail role should have the maturity to remain calm. Look for applicants who are motivated and dependable.

Establishing a Personnel File

A personnel file is a collection of paperwork about an employee's experience with your business. If you need to dismiss a worker for poor performance, detailed records can help protect you from legal action. Start a personnel file for each employee at hire. The first document to include is the completed application form.

Each personnel file should include an employee information sheet. Having contact information organized and easily available will be handy if you need to call a worker about a schedule change or provide information to an insurance company or government agency. The employee information sheet should also include the name and telephone number of someone to contact in case there is an emergency. The sample information sheet below is also found on the accompanying CD.

EMPLOYEE INFORMATION SHEET	
Applicant's last name	
First name	
Middle name	
Nickname	

EMPLOYEE INFORMATION SHEET	
Social Security Number	
Street address	
City	
State	
Zip code	
Phone number	
E-mail	
Emergency contact name	
Relationship to employee	
Telephone number	

In addition to basic employee information, file a copy of the employee's W-4 form, social security card, and driver's license. Include a signed W-9 for contract workers. Include a statement signed by the employee acknowledging receipt and review of the employee handbook.

RECEIPT OF EMPLOYEE HANDBOOK
I _____ (name of employee) received the Employee Handbook from _____ (name of supervisor) of _____ _____ (name of business). I have read the contents of the Employee Handbook and will follow the policies, procedures, and regulations.
Signed: _____ _____
Date: _____

In addition, collect employees' performance evaluations in their personnel files. Encourage employees to inform you if they move or if their contact information changes so you can keep their files up to date. When an employee leaves, note the date and reason for leaving in his or her personnel file.

Personnel files are considered confidential records. They should be kept locked, and precautions should be put in place to keep the number of people who can access them at a minimum.

Performance Evaluations

You may have employees who are not meeting your expectations, despite their desire to be good workers. Others may be ready to take on more responsibilities.

All employees have strengths and weaknesses. The most talented designer may have trouble talking with clients. Your best performing sales agent may never turn in paperwork on time. Regular performance evaluations can help employees identify areas they need to work on and give you a chance to monitor improvement.

Performance evaluations can be performed twice a year, annually, quarterly, or even monthly. Evaluations can be nerve-racking for employees, but keeping the session friendly and nonconfrontational can help reduce anxiety. Meet with each employee individually in a comfortable and private place. Assure employees that anything said during the evaluation will remain confidential.

Focus on your employee's strengths and any improved performance, but talk about areas he or she should work on. In addition, give a staff member the opportunity to talk about any concerns.

It can be helpful to give employees a copy of the performance evaluation form you will be completing. Encourage them to complete their own evaluations before their scheduled meeting times. Comparing their self-assessments to your evaluations and discussing any differences can help each party understand the other's expectations.

The following sample performance evaluation form, also found on the CD, can be used to assess your employees or as a self-evaluation tool.

PERFORMANCE EVALUATION FORM					
Employee name:					
Evaluator's name:					
Evaluator's signature:					
Date:					
Employee's signature:					
Date:					
Circle the number that best describes the employee. 1 = Never 2 = Occasionally 3 = Usually 4 = Always NA = Not Applicable					
Employee completes projects on time.	1	2	3	4	NA
Employee provides customer service according to company policy.	1	2	3	4	NA
Employee works well with other staff members.	1	2	3	4	NA
Employee accepts criticism well.	1	2	3	4	NA
Employee arrives at work and meetings on time.	1	2	3	4	NA
Employee behaves professionally.	1	2	3	4	NA
Employee understands job duties.	1	2	3	4	NA
Employee completes job duties.	1	2	3	4	NA
Employee will complete tasks outside of job description if needed.	1	2	3	4	NA
Employee continues to learn and improve job performance.	1	2	3	4	NA
Employee takes the initiative to complete routine tasks.	1	2	3	4	NA
Employee finds creative solutions to problems.	1	2	3	4	NA
Employee communicates well.	1	2	3	4	NA

PERFORMANCE EVALUATION FORM					
Employee is an effective team leader.	1	2	3	4	NA
Employee is courteous.	1	2	3	4	NA
Employee works efficiently.	1	2	3	4	NA
Employee provides thoughtful feedback.	1	2	3	4	NA
Employee displays a good attitude.	1	2	3	4	NA
Notes:					

Training a New Employee

Even if you hire an experienced designer or retailer, you will need to teach employees your company policies. A training period can also help you gauge your new employee's ability, personality, and potential.

A common training method in the fashion industry is to work on a project together with the new employee. Let your staff member perform all the job duties that relate to the project, but stay involved so that you can demonstrate your business procedures and answer any questions. For example, before assigning full responsibility for a new collection to a designer, work with him for a season. This will give you the opportunity to communicate your expectations, introduce him to the other members of your design and manufacturing team, and evaluate his work.

Keeping Qualified Staff Members

Once you find and train a good employee, you will not want to lose him or her to the competition. Keeping your staff happy can help save you money and time. Many of the steps you can take to increase employee job satisfaction cost little or no money.

Employees may find that completing the same tasks every day can become tedious. Rotating job duties or adding responsibilities can help alleviate boredom, make staff members feel appreciated, and allow your employees to gain new skills. However, workers that are placed in situations they are not qualified to handle or find their job expectations routinely changed may become stressed. Talk to your staff members before adding new duties. Make sure they are ready to take on a more challenging assignment.

Some employees may enjoy a flexible work schedule. If you allow your staff members to complete tasks at home or to access the workroom outside business hours, they will be able to fit in family responsibilities, personal appointments, or even their favorite television show. Motivated, self-starting employees are more likely to do well with a flexible work schedule. If you doubt a staff member's ability to stay focused without supervision, ease into the new schedule slowly and check to make sure key deadlines are met.

The fashion industry tends to attract creative people. Your workers may find it rewarding to have more creative freedom in their work. It can be difficult for business owners to give up authority. Whether an employee is working on a sample garment, the concept for a new line, the lineup for a fashion show, or a marketing campaign, try not to micromanage every decision. Give your employees the chance to come up with their own solutions to problems. Resist the urge to jump in at the first hint of trouble. Allow employees the opportunity to correct their mistakes. Even if employees choose to do a task differently than you would, the job can still be completed efficiently and well.

If you have industrial-grade sewing machines, your employees may enjoy using them to create or modify their own garments. If you decide to offer this perk, make sure to be clear about when the equipment will be available and for what purposes. Tell your employees if they are allowed to use your supplies or if they are expected to provide their own.

If you do not offer a competitive benefits package to your full-time employees, they may look for a company that does. In addition, benefits for part-time or contract workers can encourage talented professionals to stay with your business. Benefits can include health insurance, 401(k) retirement accounts, flexible spending accounts, and prescription packages.

One of the most obvious ways to show employees that their hard work is appreciated is to offer them more money, either in the form of a salary increase or a bonus. Monetary rewards help employees feel motivated and encourage loyalty.

If you cannot offer increased benefits or a higher salary, consider rewarding high-achieving workers with a better title. A "sales agent" promoted to "sales manager" of a region may approach her job with more energy, motivation, and drive, even if the pay remains the same.

Educational opportunities not only help your staff learn new skills and improve productivity, they can also be a motivational tool. Ambitious staff members may capitalize on the opportunity to take classes or even earn a degree with financial aid from your business. Tuition reimbursement is not the only way to offer your employees learning experiences. Some equipment suppliers will provide safety and operating classes for little or no cost. Other staff members may be willing to teach a workshop on a concept or technique. One-on-one mentoring can help young designers gain confidence and experience and will cost you nothing.

Sometimes even highly motivated employees become burnt out. They may be unable to focus on their assignments or begin to produce low-quality work. They may complain about losing their creativity and feeling disappointed in their performance. In many cases, some time away from the workroom can help rejuvenate and inspire your employees. Paid vacation time allows your staff members to step away from their work responsibility occasionally and may prevent burnout.

Some employees may enjoy the opportunity to see new cities and countries by attending trade shows or fashion events. Letting qualified staff members represent the company at functions reinforces your trust in your employees and allows you time to devote to building your business.

Employees can also be motivated by having a more comfortable or prestigious place to work. Consider rewarding hard workers by redecorating their workspaces or offices. Listen to employees' input on furniture, color schemes, and window treatments so that employees feel more attached to their surroundings.

Staff members in positions demanding creativity might lose motivation if they are swamped with paperwork, scheduling, and other routine tasks. Instead of paying a patternmaker, designer, or fashion illustrator professional rates to file invoices, make copies, and run errands, consider hiring a part-time assistant to take care of these chores and free up your staff's time. Hiring an assistant can be a good human resources tactic in addition to a smart financial move, as you are showing your employees that you recognize their time and energy is valuable.

Gifts are another common motivational tool. Presents can be given to commemorate a completed project or a year of hard work. Although some employees enjoy traditional "thank you" gifts such as fruit baskets or gift certificates, unique presents can help show your staff members that their time and talent is appreciated. Consider giving your team members limited-edition garments, jewelry, or accessories to remind them of their value to your company.

Another way to keep employees happy and productive is to provide them with the right tools they need to complete their job. High-quality, well-maintained sewing machines, design equipment, art supplies, and computers can help minimize frustration and repetitive stress injuries.

New tools and equipment can help fuel creative thinking and innovative solutions to design problems.

Particularly talented designers may be wooed by letting them design their own line or manage their own label in conjunction with your business. Employees who are tempted to leave your company in order to start their own may be tempted to stay if you make them a partner.

Protecting Your Ideas

Your employees will get to see your sample garments before they hit the stores or runways. Unethical staff members may be able to make money by copying your designs and selling them to stores or private customers themselves.

The best way to protect your work is to hire trustworthy employees and treat them fairly. Let them know that theft will not be tolerated. If copies of your designs do turn up on the market, talk with each employee individually. Try to build a family environment within your organization. Make sure your staff feels like a part of your successes and realizes that everyone is injured when someone hurts the company's profitability or image.

If you find that idea theft is a growing problem, consider consulting an attorney to see if what legal action you may be entitled to take.

Noncompete Agreements

A noncompete agreement is a contract that limits the type of work an employee can engage in after leaving a business. Some noncompete agreements say that the employee can not work for a competitor within so many years of terminating his or her relationship with the original employer. Others restrict the employee from starting a similar business or from working in the industry.

The legality of a noncompete agreement depends on your local and state laws, so make sure a lawyer reviews your terms before you require employees to sign them. If an employee signs a noncompete agreement, make sure to file a copy in his or her personnel file.

Terminations

Firing an employee is never fun, but there may come a time when it is necessary. Some common reasons staff members are fired from fashion design businesses include:

- Cash flow problems within the business

- Employee's skills are no longer needed

- Personal issues between employee and other staff members

- Personal issues between employee and owner

- Employee's performance is not meeting expectations

If you are forced to lay off employees because of unexpected expenses or because your income was less than projected, be up-front about the situation. Give your employees a reasonable estimate of when you may be able to rehire them. Offer to let them know about any job opportunities you may come across, and prepare a letter of recommendation.

If employees are no longer needed because you have decided to outsource their jobs, expect some hurt feelings. If possible, find temporary positions for them in your business while they look for another job. Remain professional and offer to assist employees however you can in their job search.

If a personal problem with the staff member is the main reason for dismissal, make sure you have exhausted all other possible remedies. Talk with everyone involved in the issue and try to open lines of communication. Work as a mediator to solve problems, and set a good example of professional conduct. Before firing an employee, give him a warning and create a plan to improve the situation. Document all your attempts to rectify the situation, and keep a copy in the employee's personnel file in case he decides to take legal action against you.

If you plan to fire employees because of their performance, try to determine possible reasons why they did not live up to your expectations. You may not have communicated the job expectations clearly during the interview. Training may have been complete or ineffective. A staff member might be having personal issues that temporarily interfere with his or her work.

Employees may not realize that you are not satisfied with their work. Talk to your staff members about any performance concerns. Make sure to document the content and outcome of each discussion. If you are unable to prove that the dismissal was warranted, you may be in violation of workers' rights laws.

Because replacing an employee can be time consuming and expensive, it may be a good idea to exhaust other possibilities before firing a staff member. Some possible ways to improve an employee's performance include:

- Help the employee stay focused and organized by writing a list of goals every day or for each project.

- Partner with a low-performing employee for a project. Demonstrate the quality of work you expect.

❧ Move the employee to another position to see if it is a better fit.

❧ Point out particular aspects of a project that should be improved. Give the employee the list in writing, and give him a chance to revise the work.

❧ Review your expectations and make sure they are appropriate for the employee's education, experience, pay rate, and work load.

❧ Issue a formal warning to the employee. The warning should say the reasons the work is unacceptable and what needs to be done to improve. Give a date by which the improvements need to be made or else the employee will be fired. Have the employee sign the warning. Give him a copy, and place a copy in his personnel file.

If you cannot improve the situation and decide the best option is to fire the employee, be sure to review your local workers' rights laws to make sure you follow the necessary procedures. An attorney or small business development center can help clarify any questions you have about the process.

It is normal to feel disappointed after a bad experience with an employee. After all, you interviewed and chose the candidate. With the right attitude, however, firing an employee can be a valuable learning experience that can improve your business. Make a list of how the employee failed to live up to your expectations. Review the employee's application and your notes of the job interview. Is there anything that could have tipped you off about potential problems? What additional questions could you have asked to learn more about the candidate? What should you look for in future applicants?

Consider the training you provided. Did it adequately prepare the employee for the demands of the position? What can you improve about the process in the future?

Investigate your business's work environment. Is it supportive and friendly, or does it encourage conflict? Do your employees have the tools and equipment they need to be successful at their jobs? Is the position's compensation package appealing?

Exit Interviews

Some of your staff members will likely leave for their own reasons. They might move with their families, find other opportunities with better compensation or more enjoyable work, decide to leave the workforce for a while, or want to start their own businesses.

Whatever the reason for their departure, you may be able to learn about their experience with your company through an exit interview. Your former employees may have good ideas about how to improve your operations.

An exit interview can be a formal meeting or an informal chat. If you think your employee may not feel comfortable talking with you, consider having another staff member conduct the interview. The comments you get will be more helpful if the employee is honest in his appraisal.

Some question that might be helpful to ask during an exit interview include:

- What inefficiencies did you experience in the business?

- What job duties were least enjoyable?

- Did you feel that your efforts were appreciated? What made you feel that way?

- What can we do to make new employees feel comfortable?

- ✦ What company policies do you not agree with? Why?

- ✦ What procedures do you feel could be streamlined?

- ✦ How could we have used your time and talent more appropriately?

- ✦ How can we provide better customer service?

- ✦ What would you tell the person who will replace you?

- ✦ What changes would you like to see made to the work environment?

- ✦ What tools or equipment would have made your job easier?

- ✦ Do you think enough time was allocated to completing projects?

- ✦ How will were your job expectations communicated to you?

- ✦ Was your compensation package appropriate for your position, education level, and experience?

Exit interviews give you a chance to identify areas in your business that are not working as well as they could be. They can also be a way to see what you are doing right.

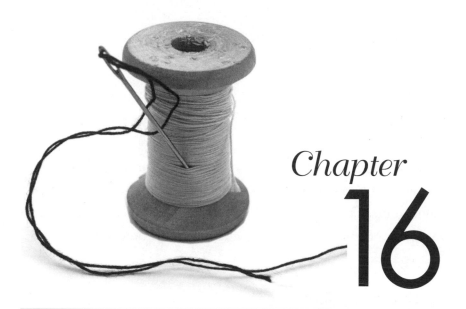

Chapter

16

Business Transactions

The fashion industry is constantly changing in response to new fibers, construction techniques, customer preferences, and cultural influences. The success of your company depends on constant evaluation of your performance, your business's profitability, and your target market's response. You may need to change your pricing, product, or marketing strategies in order to stay competitive.

Evaluating Your Performance

Many people find it difficult to appraise the quality of their own work. They are either too critical or believe that everything they turn out is perfect. If you fall into either of these categories, your business could suffer. If you constantly second-guess your work, you may find it stressful to get projects completed on time. On the other hand, if you refuse to edit your designs to match your target market's preferences, you may find it hard to sell your garments.

Your Performance as a Business Owner

As a fashion design business owner, you should regularly evaluate your performance both as a designer and as a businessperson. If you find it hard to critique yourself, consider hiring a fashion or business consultant to analyze your work and identify areas where you can improve.

Evaluating Your Designs

When critiquing a design, identify the purpose of the finished garment. Should it look sexy, sporty, quirky, playful, or professional? Consider how the garment uses design principles to achieve its purpose. How does the silhouette of the garment work with the curves and lines of the wearer? Is the volume of the garment appropriate for its intended use? What design elements are used to create visual rhythm? Is the design balanced and proportional? What is the eye drawn to when the design is first looked at? Do the color and texture of the fabric used support the image of the image you wish the design to convey? Does the design look disjointed or unified across the garment? If contrasting elements are used, are they intense enough, or do they look like mistakes?

When evaluating the designs you create, review your line as a whole in addition to each individual look. Each collection should be cohesive and have a definite point of view. Consider how the look of your line appears to your target market. Picture the people who would have every garment you design in their closets. What image would they present? Would their outfits look pulled together or disjointed?

Evaluating Your Business Skills

In addition to critiquing the designs you produce, you should evaluate your performance and growth as a businessperson. Do you treat your staff, vendors, customers, and contractors fairly? Are your records organized and up to date? Do you complete your projects or find yourself starting tasks but never quite finishing them? Are you still motivated to work on your fashion design business, or have other things become more important? Do you continue to learn about and improve your skills in marketing, accounting, and customer relations? Do you face your business-related tasks with enthusiasm?

Completing a Formal Self-Evaluation

Just as regular performance evaluations can help your employees see where they can improve, a formal self-assessment can help you identify ways you can move forward as a designer and a business owner.

The self-evaluation form below, also found on the accompanying CD, can be used to recognize your strengths and weaknesses as a business owner.

SELF-EVALUATION FORM					
Date:					
Circle the number that best describes your performance. 1 = Never 2 = Occasionally 3 = Usually 4 = Always NA = Not Applicable					
I complete the projects I start.	1	2	3	4	NA
I treat my employees, vendors, customers, and contractors fairly.	1	2	3	4	NA
I provide set company policies that are fair and well-thought-out.	1	2	3	4	NA

SELF-EVALUATION FORM					
I am an efficient and courteous leader.	1	2	3	4	NA
I provide thoughtful feedback to employees and contractors.	1	2	3	4	NA
I work well with my staff members.	1	2	3	4	NA
I accept criticism well.	1	2	3	4	NA
I arrive at work and meetings on time.	1	2	3	4	NA
My employees enjoy coming to work.	1	2	3	4	NA
I understand the roles and duties of my employees and contractors.	1	2	3	4	NA
I keep my target market in mind when creating my designs.	1	2	3	4	NA
I remain focused on the success of my business.	1	2	3	4	NA
I keep my target market in mind when devising marketing strategies.	1	2	3	4	NA
I continue to learn about and improve my design skills.	1	2	3	4	NA
I continue to learn about and improve my construction skills.	1	2	3	4	NA
I continue to learn about and improve my business skills.	1	2	3	4	NA
I take the initiative to complete routine tasks.	1	2	3	4	NA
I set a good example of professional behavior.	1	2	3	4	NA
Contractors, sales agents, and vendors enjoy working with me.	1	2	3	4	NA
I find creative solutions to problems.	1	2	3	4	NA
I communicate well.	1	2	3	4	NA
I am an effective team leader.	1	2	3	4	NA
I am courteous.	1	2	3	4	NA
I work efficiently.	1	2	3	4	NA
I provide thoughtful feedback.	1	2	3	4	NA
I have a good attitude about the fashion industry.	1	2	3	4	NA
My accounts are up to date.	1	2	3	4	NA
I fulfill orders within a reasonable time.	1	2	3	4	NA
I take responsibility for my decisions.	1	2	3	4	NA
I give back to my community.	1	2	3	4	NA

It is important to evaluate yourself at least as often as you review your employees, as it can be more difficult to see a developing problem with your own work.

Your Business's Profitability

Popular lines are not necessarily profitable. Some fashion businesses create original and creative designs and are filling new orders every day but still lose money. Careful and frequent analysis of your company's financial health can help you realize if there is a problem before the situation progresses too far to fix.

Review your budget projections and compare them with your actual income and expenses. Are you bringing in at least as much money as you hoped? Are your expenses at or below what you predicted? If you have a cash flow imbalance, try to track down the reason. If you fall short of your projections every month, recalculate your balance sheets, operating budget, and break-even analysis so you can see the middle and long-term ramifications.

Think about the following questions when reviewing your budget:

- Are you using all the features in your cell phone, Internet, or telephone plan? If not, can you downsize to a less expensive program?

- Are there supplies that you purchase every month? Can you save money by buying them in bulk less frequently?

- Are you contracting out any work that you could do as well and less expensively yourself?

- Are you running any marketing programs that are not bringing in enough sales to justify their costs?

- Are there any supplies or materials that you could purchase cheaper without compromising the quality of your garments?

🪡 Are you using the equipment and vehicles you have purchased or leased? Would it be more cost effective to rent them occasionally or contract the work out?

🪡 Is there a less expensive place from which to run your business?

🪡 Are you losing money because of a high rate of returned garments? Are there customer service or quality-control policies you can introduce in order to decrease returns?

If your business is earning more than projected, you may be tempted to increase your spending by making a large purchase or loosening your hold on expenses. Before spending the money, take the following precautions:

🪡 Review your accounts to make sure that there are no forgotten outstanding bills.

🪡 Look for any upcoming quarterly, biannual, or annual expenses. Make sure you have enough money in your budget to cover them.

🪡 Compare your ledger with your checking account statement to see if all checks have cleared.

🪡 Review the service logs of your sewing machines. Double-check that your budget includes likely upcoming maintenance costs.

🪡 Run a "worst case scenario" budget. If your current contracts are canceled and you have a large number of returns in the near future, do you have enough of a financial buffer to keep your business running?

The fashion industry can be both cyclical and fickle. Even if your income for one quarter is substantially higher than anticipated, there is no guarantee that you will continue to sell at that volume. Rather than rushing to upgrade your equipment or location, it is safer to spend money conservatively and plan for times when your income is low and expenses are high.

Your Business's Competitiveness in the Market

Financial planning often involves making assumptions about different market scenarios to predict a business's income and expenses in the future. For example, a designer who sells an innovative winter coat may run financial projections that assume the coat is the highest-selling item as well as forecasts that assume the coat is a flop.

Examining how well you are standing up against other fashion design companies who are trying to sell to the same target market can give you more insight into how well your company is likely to perform in the future. The more you understand your customers, your competition, and the way your business relates to each, the better you will be able to anticipate how well your garments will sell from season to season.

When assessing your business's market competitiveness, consider your brand awareness. Do members of your target market know your label exists? Do they prefer your garments over the competition's? Do they demand that stores carry your line?

Product availability is just as important as brand awareness. Even if customers would rather have one of your designs, if it is not available they might go with a competitor's rather than wait.

You may be losing sales to a competitor because of pricing issues. Customers do not always purchase the cheapest product. Instead, they tend to buy the garment that gives them the highest perceived value.

To analyze the price and perceived value of your designs, research competing lines and prepare a side-by-side retail price comparison. Next, correlate this chart with how well each of your designs sold and look for any patterns.

Consider a hypothetical business, White Creek Fashions, that sells mid-priced children's clothing through a regional chain and several independent boutiques. A comparison of their main competitors' fall designs and pricings is summarized in the following chart.

COMPETITIVE RETAIL PRICE COMPARISON FOR WHITE CREEK FASHIONS					
Garment	Company 1	Company 2	Company 3	Average of Competitors' Prices	White Creek Price
Toddlers' corduroys	$25	NA	$28	$26.50	$27
Toddlers' flannel 5-button shirt	$22	$24	$36	$27.33	$25
Toddlers' denim overalls	$26	$19	$45	$30	$28
Toddlers' graphic T-shirt	NA	$12	$14	$13	$10
Toddlers' fake leather jacket	$85	NA	NA	$85	$105
Toddlers' denim jacket	NA	$36	$36	$36	$28
Kids' overalls	$30	NA	$50	$40	$45
Kids' graphic T-shirt	$15	$20	$18	$17.67	$17
Kids' fake leather jacket	$95	NA	$75	$85	$115
Kids' boiled wool overcoat	NA	NA	$85	$85	$125

COMPETITIVE RETAIL PRICE COMPARISON FOR WHITE CREEK FASHIONS				
Garment	Percent Above/ Below Average Price	Projected Retail Units Sold	Actual Retail Units Sold	Percent Above/Below Projected Sales
Toddlers' corduroys	+2%	100	103	+3%
Toddlers' flannel 5-button shirt	-9%	250	285	+14%

COMPETITIVE RETAIL PRICE COMPARISON FOR WHITE CREEK FASHIONS				
Toddlers' denim overalls	-6%	100	113	+13%
Toddlers' graphic T-shirt	-23%	300	412	+37%
Toddlers' fake leather jacket	+23%	30	8	-73%
Toddlers' denim jacket	-22%	60	76	+27%
Kids' overalls	+13%	100	93	-7%
Kids' graphic T-shirt	-4%	300	298	-1%
Kids' fake leather jacket	+35%	30	3	-90%
Kids' boiled wool overcoat	+47%	15	2	-87%

The percent above/below average price of each type of garment is calculated by subtracting the average of the competitors' prices from the White Creek retail price, dividing by the average of the competitors' prices and multiplying by 100. A negative percent indicates that the White Creek price is lower than average for that kind of garment. A positive percentage indicates that the White Creek price is higher than average.

The projected retail units sold are calculated by taking a reasonable percent of the total number of garments sold to retailers. The sell-through estimates you use for your projections will vary depending on the type of clothing you sell and the retailers you sell to, but a good rule of thumb is that 50-65 percent of the garments you sell to a store will sell at full retail price.

The actual retail units sold are the numbers of each garment sold at full retail price. You can call your retailers and ask for these numbers. Sell-through is calculated by dividing the actual retail units sold by the number of garments the retailer purchased. It is a good idea to calculate and record your sell-through at each store for every season. This data will help you form more accurate projections for future sales periods.

The percent above/below projected sales column is calculated by subtracting the projected sales from the actual sales, dividing by the projected sales and multiplying by 100. A negative percent indicates that the actual sales were less than the projected sales. A positive percent means more garments were sold than expected.

In this example, pieces that were significantly higher than the competition's did not sell well. This may indicate that customers thought the garments were overpriced.

It may take a little legwork to find your competitors' retail prices. You can look at stores, Web sites, and catalogs that carry their designs. If you find a wide variety of retail prices for an identical garment, use an average or use the price from the store whose clientele is most like yours in age, economic status, location, and buying preference.

Pricing and sell-through analyses can help you determine how well you understand your selected niche. In the White Creek Fashions example, the designer thought there would be a demand within her target market for formal outerwear for children. Her research indicated that the children in her target market dressed up for church, parties, and other special occasions. She determined that parents would be delighted with an alternative to ski jackets and parkas.

White Creck's lowest performers, however, were the formal outerwear designs. Once the owner notices this trend, she can reevaluate whether the garments have a place in the line. If she decides to keep them, she might need to research her target market more in order to tweak the design and make it have a higher perceived value.

There are several possible reasons why a design might not sell as well as expected:

🌢 **The target market does not need or want the garment**. Evening wear, business suits, and exercise outfits are notorious low performers in certain populations. If you have excess inventory of an underperforming garment and expect that this is the reason, consider selling it outside your usual target market.

🍂 **Customers do not need the garment enough to justify the price.** In the White Creek Fashions example, the parents may like the idea of formal outwear for their children, but they did not want to pay more than $100 for a garment that would be worn only once or twice for one season. If White Creek made the coats with cheaper materials, they might be able to bring the price down enough to tempt more people to buy them and still have a reasonable profit margin.

🍂 **Customers do not know the garment exists.** If people do not know about your design, they cannot actively look for it. Whether you sell your garments to retail stores or directly to consumers, you need to let your customers know what you have available and how they can complete purchases. Ineffective communication can lead to poor sales.

🍂 **Customers are unable to buy the garment.** Even if your target market knows about, wants, and is willing to pay for your designs, your garments will not sell if your customers are not able to find them. If you believe this is the case, review your distribution channels. Are you placing your designs in stores where your intended customers are likely to shop? Is your Web site easy to find and navigate? Have you manufactured enough garments to meet demand? Do you accept different types of payment? Do your payment, return, or shipping policies dissuade buyers?

🍂 **Customers had a bad previous experience with similar designs.** An athlete who had an expensive pair of running pants fall apart after one washing might be hesitant to buy another pair constructed from the same material, even if the garment is designed and manufactured by a different company. If you suspect a competitor's product has biased your target market against your designs, consider positioning your designs as high-quality alternatives that live up to the promises others failed to deliver.

🖈 **Customers have heard bad things about your company or designs**. The Internet has made it easy for retail businesses and consumers to research products before they make a purchase. Some niche markets are small and close knit. After one person's bad experience is shared, discussed, and recounted, you may lose a significant number of sales. It is difficult but not impossible to fix your reputation. One option is to focus on a different target market. Another choice is to segment your current market and focus on customers who either do not know about your product or who do not care what other people say or think about your brand. However you decide to address the issue, remember to address the underlying causes of your poor reputation.

🖈 **Customers had a bad previous experience with your company**. Consumers can have long memories when it comes to fashion. If they were not satisfied with your garments or customer service, they might be hesitant to buy your designs again. One way to handle this situation is to face the problem head on. Explain to unsatisfied customers what you have done to make their future experiences with your company better. Invite them to give you another chance to earn their loyalty. Consider adding a financial incentive such as a coupon or gift certificate.

Setting Goals

Evaluating your performance, profitability, and competitiveness can help identify areas where you need work. Defining and working toward goals can help you strengthen problem areas.

Most people are more likely to reach their goals if the goals are concrete, in writing, and have a defined time. A goal like "become a better sewer" is vague and open ended, but a specific plan with a deadline, for example "complete a couture finishing technique class this spring," describes a destination that can be reached.

Goal setting is an ongoing process. To keep your business moving forward, you should have short-term, middle-term, and long-term goals. Short-term goals are those that will be completed within a few days or weeks. These usually focus on the day-to-day business tasks. Middle-term goals may take several months to reach and include seasonal objectives. Long-term goals are the strategic plans you have for the upcoming years.

Planning for the future security of your company can be daunting. One way to make long-term goals more manageable is to break them into middle- and short-term goals as in the following example. A blank version of the form used in the example is found on the accompanying CD.

WHITE CREEK FASHIONS — GOAL PLANNING FORM		
Long-term Goals	Middle-term Goals	Short-term Goals
Long-term goal: Increase sell-through of toddler and kids' formal outerwear to 60% by 12/31/2008.		
	Decrease production costs of fake leather jackets and overcoats.	
		Research alternative materials for overcoats.
		Revise design of fake leather jacket to reduce details.
		Renegotiate production terms with manufacturer.
	Improve market awareness of designs.	
		Participate in back-to-school fashion shows in towns where White Creek has a retail presence.
		Purchase full-page ad in a regional parenting magazine.
		Publicize sponsorship of local coat drives.
Long-term goal: Increase wholesale income by 50% by 2012.		

WHITE CREEK FASHIONS — GOAL PLANNING FORM		
	Introduce coordinating adult clothing.	
		Research market interest in coordinating clothing.
		Decide where to focus initial efforts in coordinated clothing: outerwear or casual shirts.
		Select three or four designs from current collection to interpret into men's wear and ladies' fashions.
		Design adult interpretations of selected garments and add to current marketing materials.
	Increase sales of juvenile sportswear and outerwear by 50%.	
		Identify possible sportswear and outerwear additions to current collection.
		Research current market to determine which possible additions are most likely to be successful.
		Select three or four additional garments to add to current collection.
		Design additional juvenile sportswear and outerwear garments and add to current marketing materials.
	Increase number of distribution outlets by 50%	
		Renegotiate sales region with representative.
		If necessary, hire additional sales staff.
		Expand sales area to include the entire Midwest by showing the line at industry events throughout the region.

Adapting Business Strategies

One of the benefits of constantly and consistently evaluating the state of your business is that it gives you a chance to identify and fix small issues before they become large problems.

If you are concerned about your business's cash flow or performance, you may need to adjust your pricing strategies, product line, marketing plan, or business policies.

Adjusting Pricing Strategies

A common mistake for new business owners is to cut prices at the first sign of financial trouble. The simple supply-and-demand models taught in introductory business courses suggests that when price is lowered, more units are sold. Fledgling fashion designers may be tempted to undercut their competitors in the hope of signing a larger sales contract.

In most fashion circles, cheaper designs do not necessarily sell better. Whether you are selling to retailers or consumers, your customers are more likely to purchase the garments they perceive as being a better value. To retailers, value is determined by how easily they think they can make a profit. To consumers, value often means how much enjoyment or utility they will get from the clothing.

Raising the price of your garments can benefit your bottom line in several ways. By charging more per piece, you will raise your profit margin. Elementary economics says that at higher prices, fewer garments will be sold. However, to fashion consumers a bigger price tag may make a design more appealing. Higher-priced items are more likely to be seen as exclusive, well-made and desirable. Some customers, both retail and wholesale, do not want to have the same merchandise that is carried by discount stores. By increasing your prices, you might even sell more garments.

For every design, there is a price point where the average customers decide the benefits of the garment are not worth the cost. If you are pricing your line above this point, sales will decrease. In this case, you can either reduce your price or adjust your marketing strategy to make your target customers more enthusiastic about the benefits of your merchandise.

Lowering your prices does come with some risks. A price cut tarnishes the image of an exclusive, expensive line. In addition, it might make customers who purchased the garments at a higher price feel that they had spent their money poorly.

Adjusting Your Line

If your designs do not connect with your customers, you will have slow sales no matter how you price your garments. There are several reasons why your line may not resonate with your target market. A design element may be at fault. Customers may not like the color, pattern, texture, or detailing of a garment.

The types of garments or materials used to construct your pieces may not fit with your customers' life styles. Some people will avoid clothing that needs to be dry cleaned or ironed. Women who do not attend many evening functions may need only one or two formal dresses in their closets. Men tend to buy suits less often than they purchase jeans, T-shirts and other casual wear. If your line is filled with garments that people rarely buy, you may need to fill it out with more popular designs to improve your cash flow.

If you suspect that your sales could be improved by adjusting or adding to your line, consult your sales representatives, wholesale buyers, or retail sales staff. They may have a better understanding of what your target market is looking for.

Interviews and surveys can also give you insight into your target market's purchasing behavior. Interviews can either be informal talks with the customers you want your designs to appeal to or structured meetings with a set list of questions. Interviews can be conducted one-on-one or as a focus group of several customers.

Interviewers usually ask open-ended questions and may record the interviewees' responses verbatim or take notes on key topics. Interviewers may deviate from the prepared questions if a customer's response brings up a new topic or idea.

Surveys can be conducted in person, through the mail, by telephone, or over the Internet. Because surveys use short-answer questions, they may not provide as detailed information as interviews. They may be more cost-effective than either focus groups or one-on-one interviews.

When preparing an interview or survey, know that the more time it takes customers to complete the questions, the less likely they will be to participate. Customers may be more eager to help if they are offered some sort of premium, such as a gift certificate, accessory, or coupon, in exchange for answering the questions.

Possible interview and survey questions are listed in the chart below.

SAMPLE MARKETING QUESTIONS	
Interview Questions	**Survey Questions**
What kind of outfits do you prefer to wear to work?	How many skirts do you expect to buy during the next six months?
How do you launder your favorite outfit?	How often do you use a dry cleaning service?
What colors to you like to wear?	Do you wear pastels, jewel tones, or neutrals?
How does your working wardrobe differ from your weekend clothes?	Do you prefer to wear a suit or separates to work?
What clothing features would you be willing to pay more for?	How much do you usually pay for a shirt?
How would you describe your personal style?	Where do you usually shop for clothing?
What do you think makes a high-quality article of clothing?	Would you rather have a few high-quality outfits or many cheaper pieces?

Adjusting Marketing Strategies

Even if you understand your target customers' preferences, if you are unable to communicate the features and benefits of your line you may experience disappointing sales.

Some marketing strategies are too vague to be effective. Rather than narrowing in on the line's benefits as they apply to the target market, they are centered on the design's features. In fashion, not everyone is a potential customer. Some groups shy away from classic designs; others embrace them. Some consumers want cutting-edge looks; others prize comfort over style. If you are trying to market your clothing indiscriminately, you may not be getting the most from your advertising budget.

An advertising campaign can also be too specific and alienate potential customers. If your marketing materials use symbolism, descriptions, or images that are offensive to people who might otherwise be interested in your garments, you may be losing sales. Although finding a niche is an important step in building a fashion design business, if you broaden your target market slightly, you might find new customers. Consider a designer who creates tai chi outfits from recycled cotton. He may expand his business if he markets his designs as a unique, comfortable, and environmentally friendly loungewear in addition to selling them to tai chi practitioners.

Even the most thoughtful, well-designed marketing campaign cannot be effective if it does not reach enough customers. If this is your situation, you may need to invest more money in your current direct mailings, sales trips, and online promotions.

Some possible ways to jump-start your marketing performance include:

- **Reevaluating the appropriateness of the magazines** that run your advertisements. Magazines change their focus and target audience just like fashion designers do. If your advertising campaign has become less effective, check with the periodical's marketing department to see if the demographics of its readers have shifted.

❧ **Look at your advertisements with a critical eye**, or hire a consultant to critique them. If your ad style is dated, you will not be able to communicate the intended image of your clothing line to your target market.

❧ **Review your special events calendar**. Determine if you have scheduled enough public and media relations activities and if the activities are the type that will reach your potential customers.

❧ **Think about your Web site**. Are there enough features to attract and hold the attention of visitors? Do the graphics load quickly? If people have to wait to see your fashions, they are likely to click away from your site. Do the applications run on all major Web browsers and operating systems?

❧ **If you are using keyword advertising** to draw visitors to your Web site, analyze the performance of each campaign. Are you allocating your online marketing funds as effectively as possible?

Adjusting Policies

Customers who had a bad service experience with a company are less likely to buy from that business again. This includes wholesale buyers, who probably have a variety of suppliers competing for limited rack and shelf space, as well as retail customers.

Customer service policies should be written to make the purchasing process as trouble-free as possible. Unfortunately, some policies do the opposite.

Some customer service policies that might be hurting your sales include:

- **Overly restrictive return requirements**. It is common to set a time limit on returns and require the garment be in unused condition before issuing a refund. If the time limit is less than two weeks or if you require that excessive paperwork accompanies returned items, customers may avoid buying from you in the future.

- **Unrealistic marketing and resell conditions**. Although it is acceptable to protect your line's image by setting some restrictions about how retailers can display, sell, and advertise your garments, your buyers may find other vendors if their merchandising options are too limited. If you wholesale your designs, avoid micromanaging your retailers. Limit your conditions to practices that are not likely to damage your future sales.

- **Slow or limited communication**. Customers should be able to reach you about their questions and concerns. If you cannot afford a customer service representative or receptionist to answer the telephone, invest in an answering machine. Check it often and return calls promptly. Be sure you have an e-mail address for customers who prefer to communicate over the Internet. Try to answer all inquiries within a few hours.

Some employment policies can also affect your sales. If your staff is not happy, customer service and product quality may suffer.

Human resource policies that may decrease your profitability include:

- **Inadequate compensation**. Employees want to feel valued and appreciated. If you pay minimum wage and offer no benefits, you are sending the message that your staff members are replaceable and unskilled. Likewise, the job is replaceable. This can cultivate an environment where personnel do not care about the service they provide. If the company does not make money or even fails, employees know that they can find another low-paying job. There is no incentive to help the business succeed. Inadequate compensation can also result in high staff turnover, which means you are constantly looking for and training new staff members.

❧ **Poor training**. A staff member who does not know your business policies and procedures will be unable to follow them. If there is no consistency in sales, return, and ordering procedures, vendors and customers can become confused and irritated.

❧ **Inflexible scheduling**. Employees have lives outside your fashion design business. If you encourage them to attend occasional school events, doctor appointments, and personal meetings during business hours, your staff members are likely to be more relaxed and productive while they are working.

How you treat your vendors and contractors can also affect the success of your business. Some mills and manufacturers are hesitant to work with small fashion design businesses. Small orders often mean reduced profit margins. In addition, fashion is a volatile industry, and new companies may go out of business before bills are paid.

Once a supplier or contractor agrees to work with you, make sure your policies do not make them regret the decision. Treat your vendors and contractors professionally. Pay invoices on time. Do not invent reasons to return merchandise. Do not expect your contractors to rearrange their schedules because you are behind or agreed to a tight deadline.

Securing Continued Financing

After assessing your business's situation, you may decide that you need additional money in order to fix marketing or customer service problems, increase production, expand your line, or boost product quality. If you do not have the personal funds to invest in your company, a business loan may be a good choice.

If you need additional financing because you are having trouble paying your operational expenses, your options might be limited. Banks and lending institutions are not likely to make you a loan in this situation because they fear the loan payment will only increase your operational deficit.

However, they may be able to extend credit if you can prove that your money shortage is a temporary situation. For example, you may need money to purchase supplies for the next season's line while you wait for customers to pay their bills. If you can demonstrate you will be able to repay them, creditors may offer you a loan or revolving line of credit to tide you over.

Most lenders prefer to work with established, profitable businesses that need money to grow. As you gain experience with your fashion design business, you may find that you need specialized equipment, a location that will attract more clients, or more room to work. If you need money to fund a major purchase that will increase your business's profitability, lenders will want to see evidence that you have researched the purchase and firm numbers that show you are a good credit risk.

Applying for a Loan

When you apply for a loan, bankers are most interested in the following key questions:

- How much money do you need?

- How will you use the money?

✦ How will you pay back the money?

✦ Do you have a history of repaying loans?

✦ What collateral can you offer?

✦ How much equity is in the business?

Lenders will want to know about what your business does, how many people you employ, and how much money you bring in through sales every year. They will want to refer to your business's financial statements in addition to personal financial statements of the owners, officers, and major stockholders.

The collateral you offer can be the deciding factor in whether you get a loan. Collateral is property that is used to secure a loan. If you default on the loan, the lenders can sell the collateral to help recoup their losses. It is common for lenders to accept the following as collateral:

✦ Real estate   ✦ Receivables

✦ Trucks   ✦ Industrial equipment

✦ Furniture   ✦ Financial CDs

✦ Stocks   ✦ Bonds

Lenders will not usually accept:

✦ Cars   ✦ Perishables

✦ Jewelry   ✦ Office equipment

✦ IRAs   ✦ Mutual funds

Funding Application Checklist

Before you apply for a business loan, make sure you have updated copies of the common supporting materials loan officers ask for.

BUSINESS LOAN APPLICATION CHECKLIST	
	Business profile
	The purpose, amount, and type of loan you want
	Collateral offered
	Balance sheets for the past three years
	Profit-loss statements for the past three years
	List of accounts receivable
	Personal asset and liability lists for owners
	Owners' personal tax returns for the past three years
	Résumés for owners, key personnel, and officers
	Competition analysis
	Market analysis
	Loan break-even analysis

Funding Application Schedule

From the time you apply for a loan until you receive a check from the bank can take up to three months. Although the loan application process can differ depending on the bank, most institutions follow the same basic procedures.

BUSINESS LOAN SCHEDULE	
Approximate Time Required	Description
1 to 2 weeks	Review the business plan checklist and gather the paperwork and business information you will need. If you have an updated business plan, most of the information should be there.

BUSINESS LOAN SCHEDULE	
2 to 3 weeks	If the loan is for a major equipment or real estate purchase, negotiate sale terms and obtain a copy of the purchase agreement.
5 to 7 days	Schedule an appointment with a representative from the bank or lending institution.
1 week	Meet with the lender. Bring a list of questions you want to ask. Find out about any additional application requirements and complete a formal application.
1 to 5 days	Turn in any additional information that the lender has requested.
1 to 2 weeks	Wait for the lender's response.
1 week	Review the lender's approval or denial letter. If you are approved and decide to take the loan, sign and return the commitment letter. Schedule the loan closing.
1 week	If you are applying for an SBA loan, complete the required paperwork.
30 to 45 days	Sign the final loan papers at the loan closing.

Once you have secured a business loan, be sure to make your payments on time. If you apply for additional funds in the future, loan officers will review your past payment history. A string of late or missing payments may make it more difficult to get approved.

Financial Emergencies

Fashion design businesses are especially vulnerable to surprise financial shortfall. Trends can change quickly, and designs that were best-sellers early in the season can be outdated and on the clearance rack a few weeks later.

Designers should plan for periodic financial shortfalls, but even the most conscientious business owner may experience the occasional economic emergency. If you are short on money because of unforeseen factors, it may be difficult to apply for and receive a business loan quickly.

Business owners who need to improve cash flow immediately have several options.

Sell Assets and Inventory

One way to increase short-term income is to sell your equipment, inventory, supplies, or samples. You may have a backup sewing machine in a storage cabinet, or samples of designs that you no longer sell. If you set your purchasing price below market value, you may be able to sell your goods rapidly.

Before you decide to sell any assets, determine if you will need them to operate your business. If you will, calculate how much it will take to replace them. Be careful about unloading sewing machines, computers, and other equipment that you will have to buy again. You may be losing money in the long term.

Avoid liquidating inventory that you will need to fill open orders. Try not to sell current designs to off-price retailers. Even if it does not violate the terms of your sales agreement with other retailers, it may devalue your designs and decrease your ability to sell to department stores and boutiques in the future.

Lines of Credit

A business line of credit can help you pay bills, make payroll, or buy equipment. Credit lines may be easier to apply for and receive than business loans and have higher limits and lower interest rates than credit cards. Most lines of credit are unsecured so you do not have to offer the lender collateral. Some lines of credit have interest-only payment options. Although this allows more flexibility in how much you pay, if you wrack up significant debt without paying down the balance, you may be adding to your business's financial difficulties.

Credit Cards

Credit cards are easier to obtain than business loans or lines of credit. The credit limit and interest rate depends on your credit rating. Credit card approval usually does not depend on having collateral, although there are secured credit card programs available to help applicants improve their poor credit scores.

Credit cards usually have higher interest rates than lines of credit or business loans. Like lines of credit, credit card balances can be difficult to pay off if you often elect to pay only the minimum, interest-only payment.

Personal Loans

A loan from a friend, family member, or even employee can help make ends meet during times of financial hardship. Personal loans can have low interest rates and flexible repayment terms. However, they can also be the source of hurt feelings and resentment. The lender may think he is entitled to give advice or make business decisions because of the loan. If the loan is not repaid according to schedule, the personal relationship may suffer.

Reduce Expenses

You may be able to improve your income by decreasing your short-term outlays. List your standing supply orders and cancel any that are not critical to keep your business running. If you are renting sewing, knitting, or embroidery machines, review the contracts and see if you can return any equipment without penalty. Even if you are in the habit of paying bills as soon as they arrive, look at the due dates on your invoices carefully. You may be able to put off paying some for 30, 60, or even 90 days.

Leaving the Business

Some fashion design business owners operate and grow their operations until they die, but many will decide to leave. Although some businesses will fail financially, there are many other reasons businesses close. Some owners grow bored with designing, manufacturing, or selling. Some may want to explore other interests.

If you decide to leave your business, you need to decide whether to try to sell the company to a new owner or to simply close the doors.

Selling the Business

You may be able to sell your business to an employee, a competitor, an investor, or another fashion designer. If you cannot find a buyer yourself, a business broker may be able to connect you with an interested buyer.

There are many factors that will contribute to your ability to sell your fashion design business. These include your business's:

- Reputation in the industry
- Open contracts
- Accounts payable
- Equity
- Amount of outstanding debt
- Accounts receivable
- Assets
- Current market preferences

- Inventory
- Liabilities
- Cash flow
- Market outlook
- Staff experience and expertise

If there is a market for your business, selling it can help you recover the losses you may have incurred in starting or operating your business. If your business has already broken even, the sale may help finance your next business venture.

What is Your Business Worth?

Once you have a potential buyer for your company, you need to decide on the sale terms. Prepare yourself for the contract negotiations by preparing the following financial reports:

- Balance sheet
- Cash flow report
- Profit and loss statement
- Accounts payable report
- Accounts receivable report

Balance Sheet

A balance sheet is a list of a business's liabilities and assets. Information on the balance sheet is used to calculate the net working capital ratio, an important number used for valuing your business.

The net working capital ratio shows a business's ability to pay its short-term bills. It is calculated by dividing current assets by current liabilities. If your current assets are $19,000 and your current liabilities total $17,800, then your net working capital ratio is 19,000 divided by 17,800, or 1.07.

A net working capital ratio greater than 1.1 indicates a healthy business. If the ratio is less than 1.1, the business may have trouble meeting its short-term obligations.

Cash Flow Report

Cash flow reports list all business income and expenses. Potential buyers will want to see that more money is coming into the business than leaving it.

Profit and Loss Statement

A profit and loss statement summarizes whether a business is making or losing money. Unlike a balance sheet, a profit and loss statement does not list business assets.

Accounts Payable Report

An accounts payable report lists all the business's outstanding bills. It should include the amount of the bill, the date it is due, and the contact information of the payee.

Accounts Receivable Report

Depending on your sales contracts, your buyers may have several weeks or even months to pay the balance of their bills. The accounts receivable report details the money that is owed to the business.

Setting a price for your business can be difficult. Although financial statements can give you and prospective buyers an overview of the financial health of a business, it can not price intangible assets such as reputation, expertise, uniqueness, image, and brand recognition. External conditions, such as the number of other fashion design businesses on the market, the health of the local and national economy, and the demographics of the target market will also influence the value of your business.

Potential buyers may be interested in one thing — the business's ability to make money. A professional business appraiser can help you calculate a reasonable price for your business.

Legal Considerations

Make sure that any information you give potential buyers when evaluating your business or negotiating sales details is accurate and complete. Any errors, even if they are unintentional, may make you vulnerable to a lawsuit. If you have any doubt about the validity of your numbers, consider hiring an accountant or lawyer to review your calculations.

Depending on your sales terms, you may not be able to step away from the business after you sign the contract. The buyer may require that you provide training or consultation services for a time period after the transfer of ownership. Some sales agreements limit the seller's ability to open, operate, or work for a competing design business.

You may also wish to add some conditions to the sales contract. For example, you may want to negotiate a buy-back clause in case you regret selling the business. In addition, you may want to reserve certain trademarks or creative property.

As with any business deal, make sure you have read and understand all the terms of the sale before signing the contract. Consider having your own lawyer review the contract. Do not rely on the buyer's, broker's, or sales agent's interpretations or assurances that certain terms will not be enforced.

Tax Considerations

You may not be able to pocket the entire purchase price of your business. The government is likely to want a significant chunk of your profit in the form of taxes. The amount of taxes you will need to pay following the sale of your business will depend on several factors, including the company structure, how the purchase price was calculated, and the value of the transferred assets.

If your company is a business or sole proprietorship, the money you receive from selling the business will be treated as personal income. If you are selling an S Corporation, your taxes will depend on whether you sell the assets or stock of your company. Usually only the stock of a C Corporation is sold to reduce the taxes.

Certain contract terms will place more of the tax burden for the sale on the seller. For example, if you agree to stay with the business as a business, marketing, or fashion consultant, then you may have to pay increased earned income taxes.

The tax considerations of selling your business are complex and subject to change from year to year. An accountant, tax advisor, or attorney can help you estimate the tax bill from a sales agreement and identify ways to minimize your cost.

Obligations to Your Successor

Buyers are often eager to add agreements to the sales contract that require the seller to work as a consultant for a time. This setup can have tax benefits for the buyer. In addition, employees, vendors, contractors, and clients may be more willing to remain with the company if the operations seem consistent, despite the change in ownership. New business owners may also recognize that they do not know much about running a fashion design business. By learning from the previous owners' experience, they may save time, money, and frustration.

There are many reasons you might agree to remain involved with the company after the sale is final. The buyer may settle on a higher price for the business because you will be there to guide and help him. Even if you are ready to step away from the responsibilities and stress of owning a fashion design business, you may not want to completely leave the industry or the label you created. Perhaps you are just not the type of person who enjoys too much free time, and you are eager to have another project to work on.

Even if the sales contract does spell out specific requirements for you during the transition period, you should plan to do the following:

- Discuss your employees' future with the buyer and develop a transition plan.

- Encourage the buyer to spend time at the business location to observe the operations.

- Tell your employees that you will be leaving the business and explain how the change will likely affect their jobs.

- Organize your employee, financial, and project files.

- Introduce the new owners to your staff.

- Explain to vendors, contractors, and clients that the business is under new management.

- If the new owner will be operating the business from the same location, remove your personal belongings.

- If you will be shipping equipment, lock down any moving parts and wrap fragile sections with cloth or bubble wrap. Include the manuals and maintenance logs.

- Prepare a contact list of your vendors, contractors, and clients.

- Make a list of any login names and passwords the new owner will need to access online records or accounts.

It is a good idea to stay friendly and professional with the new owner during and after the transition period. There may be a time when you want to work with the new owner on a project or need a business recommendation. You may find that you miss being involved with the business you started. Your buyer is more likely to help you if you left the business organized and prepared for the new owner.

Obligations to Your Employees

Your employees may have different reactions to learning that you have sold, or are trying to sell, the business. Some may be scared about how the change will affect their positions, salaries, benefits, and working environment. Others might miss you on a personal level. Employees that find out about the sale through a vendor, client, or contractor may feel betrayed and angry.

After you decide to sell your business, one of the first decisions you need to make is when to tell your employees. You probably do not need to tell your staff the minute you start to think about a private sale, especially if you have not decided to go through with it. By the time you start to show the business to prospective buyers, however, your employees are likely to suspect that something is happening. Try to explain the situation to your staff before gossip and fear disrupt the workplace and decrease productivity.

You can discuss the sale with your employees as a group or during individual meetings. The best choice for your business depends on the dynamics and size of your work force. Be honest with your staff. Come prepared to answer the following questions:

- Why are you selling the business?

- Will you close the business if it does not sell?

- Will you consider selling the business to an employee or group of employees?

- When do you think the sale will go through?

- What will happen to the employees if you sell the business?

- Are you trying to sell the entire business or just the assets?

- What will happen to the projects we are working on?

- Will you provide recommendations to employees who do not stay with the new owners?

- Will you provide any sort of severance package?

- Is the business in financial trouble?

- Will the design focus of the business change?

🖋 Will you be starting another line?

Although you are not obligated to give your employees all the information they ask for, avoid lying to them. If you do not know the buyer's plans for your staff, do not assure your employees that their jobs are safe. Even if you rationalize that you are saving them from worry and stress, you are decreasing the time they have to look for new positions.

Closing the Business

If you cannot find a suitable buyer or if you do not think you will make enough money to justify the work needed to sell your business, you may decide to simply close your business and cease designing, producing, and selling garments under that label.

Settling Accounts

Expect contractors, suppliers, and lenders who hear about your impending closure to be concerned about their outstanding bills. You may need to work out a payment plan or arrange for the transfer of collateral with your creditors.

Review your accounts receivable and try to collect any unpaid invoices. If necessary, contact a lawyer about how to handle bills that are not due until after your closing date.

Close your business's bank and credit card accounts.

Informing Employees

You should let your employees know that you will be closing the business as soon as it is a certainty. Give them as much time as possible to find another job. If you are offering a severance package, put the details in writing. Find out how employees can continue with their insurance plans. Use your contacts in the industry to help your staff members connect with new job opportunities. Check with your state business office or secretary of state to see if you need to pay employees for any unused vacation days.

Asset Liquidation

You may need to sell your equipment, property, and leftover inventory in order to pay your unresolved bills or fill outstanding orders. Competitors and equipment dealers may want to purchase your sewing machines and fixtures. Your sales representative may be able to sell your excess inventory or samples to off-price realtors.

Some businesses contract with auctioneers or liquidators to sell remaining property. Be sure not to sell any property that stands as collateral for a loan until the loan has been completely repaid.

Legal Requirements

The procedure for closing your business depends on the structure of your company. For a sole proprietorship with no employees, you will need to settle your current accounts; liquidate your equipment, inventory, and other assets; and cancel your business licenses.

If you have any employees, you will need to file an employment tax form and indicate that this is your last filing. In addition, each employee will need a final W-2 (Wage and Tax Statement) and Form 5500 (Annual Return/Report of Employee Benefit Plan). Each independent contractor should be issued a completed 1099-MISC. File Form W-3 (Transmittal of Income and Tax Statements) and Form 1096 (Annual Summary and Transmittal of U.S. Information Returns) with the IRS.

Partnerships and corporations have additional legal and tax obligations. You will have to file your federal tax returns and pay any outstanding taxes. Indicate to the IRS that this is your final return by checking the appropriate box on the form. You will also need to report any capital gains or losses using Form 1040 (Individual Income Tax Return), Form 1065 (Partnership Return of Income), or Form 1120 Schedule D (Capital Gains and Losses).

In addition, partnerships should file Form 11065 Schedule K-1 (Partner's Share of Income, Credits, Deductions, etc.). Corporation shareholders will need to file Form 1120S Schedule K-1 (Shareholder's Share of Income, Credits, Deductions, etc.). Corporations formally report their closing using Form 966 (Corporate Dissolution or Liquidation).

If you sell or exchange any assets, you may need to file Form 8594 (Asset Acquisition Statement) or Form 4797 (Sale of Business Property).

Regardless of the structure of your company, check with your state and local business authorities to see if there are any additional requirements.

The Next Step

Whether you are leaving your business for financial, personal, or professional reasons, you are likely to have mixed feelings about the transition. You have probably invested a significant amount of time, money, and creative energy in your business and your designs. If you plan to jump into another business venture, take some time to think about what went right and what went wrong with your fashion design business. List what you would change about the experience.

If you will still be involved with the business as an employee or consultant, you may find it difficult to no longer guide the company's strategic decisions. You may even regret your decision to sell the company. Try to remember the reasons you had for changing your role in the business. It may help to distance yourself from operations as much as possible. If you still cannot shake your regret, consider approaching the new owner about selling the business back to you or allowing you to buy in as a partner. You may find professional satisfaction in starting a new fashion design business, as long as it does not violate your sales agreement.

Opening and operating a successful business can take as much creativity as developing a fashion line. You must carve out a niche in your target market, find ways to advertising your designs, and develop an appropriate image. Recognize the effort it took to build your company. If possible, take some time off to recharge your artistic batteries before jumping into a new project.

CASE STUDY: MARGARET EGOROVA

Margaret Egorova, Dancer and Costume Designer

To me, the most important consideration when designing costumes is to find a fabric that is comfortable for the dancers and allows them to fulfill the movements set by the choreographer.

I try to learn as much as I can about the choreography and the dancers. The materials I use depend on the concept of the piece. If you need a flowing and airy look, you might use chiffon skirts. I recently designed for a project set in the Depression Era, and I used pinstripe pants and men's undershirts to set a serious, sad tone. I try to avoid tight knits unless the piece is very conceptual. They have no flow and do not move with the dancer.

When I was training as a dancer, my teachers would allow us to wear only tights and leotards. When I danced, I was very aware of my appearance and would wonder what was jiggling and if I was showing too much. I felt that I was not able to perform up to my potential because I was so uncomfortable. Because of this, I always try to design costumes that the dancers will enjoy dancing in.

Conclusion

The fashion industry has come a long way since the Chambre Syndicale de la Couture Parisienne was founded in 1868. New fibers, fabrics, and blends will continue to expand designers' choices and ability to meet consumer needs. The more you learn about your target market, garment construction, and business operations, the better prepared you will be to use these innovations and grow your fashion design business.

Bibliography

Allen, Anne and Julian Seaman. *Fashion Drawing: Basic Principles*. London: B.T. Batsford Ltd, 1993.

Bly, Robert W. *The Copywriter's Handbook*. New York: Henry Holt and Company, 2005.

Brown, Gordon, Paul Sukys and Mary Ann Lawlor. *Business Law with UCC Applications*. 8th ed. Westerville, OH: McGraw-Hill, 1995.

Bureau of Consumer Protection, Federal Trade Commission. *Threading Your Way Through the Labeling Requirements Under the Textile and Wool Acts*. 2005.

Bureau of Labor Statistics, U.S. Department of Labor. *Occupational Outlook Handbook*. 2006-07 Edition.

Burns, Leslie Davis and Nancy O. Bryant. *The Business of Fashion*. 2nd ed. Fairchild Publications, 2002.

Gehlhar, Mary. *The Fashion Designer Survival Guide*. New York: Kaplan Publishing, 2005.

Harder, Francis. *Fashion for Profit*. Rolling Hills Estates, CA: Harder Publications, 2000.

Kendall, Kenneth and Julie E. Kendall. *Systems Analysis and Design*. 4th ed. Upper Saddle River, NJ: Prentice-Hall, 1999.

Kloss, Dagmar. *The Dyer's Companion*. Loveland, CO: Interweave Press, 2004.

Kotler, Philip and Gary Armstrong. *Principles of Marketing*. 11th ed. Upper Saddle River, NJ: Prentice-Hall, 2006.

Lauer, David and Stephen Pentak. *Design Basics*. 5th ed. Orlando, FL: Harcourt Brace, 2000.

Menz, Deb. *Color Works*. Loveland, CO: Interweave Press, 2004.

Mulvagh, Jane. *Vogue History of 20th Century Fashion*. London: Penguin Books, 1988.

Nickerson, Robert. *Business and Information Systems*. 2nd ed. Upper Saddle River, NJ: Prentice-Hall, 2001.

Parker, Roger. *Looking Good in Print*. 5th ed. Scottsdale, AZ: Paraglyph Press, 2003.

Pinson, Linda. *Anatomy of a Business Plan*. 5th ed. Chicago: Dearborn Trade Publishing, 2001.

Shaeffer, Claire B. *High Fashion Sewing Secrets from the World's Best Designers*. Emmaus, PA: Rodale Press, 1997.

Stoughton, Mary. *Substance and Style*. Alexandria, VA: EEI Press, 2004.

Thornton, Nellie. *Fashion for Disabled People*. London: B.T. Batsford Ltd, 1990.

Williams, Robin. *The Non-Designer's Design Book*. 2nd ed. Berkeley, CA: Peachpit Press, 2004.

Author Dedication & Biography

"I would like to thank all the designers and fashion professionals who took time from their busy lives to be interviewed for this book, Angela Adams at Atlantic Publishing for her help and for giving me so much freedom to explore this topic, the drive-through crews at my local fast-food restaurants for keeping me supplied with caffeinated beverages, and my husband David for his encouragement."

In addition to writing about business and science topics, Janet Engle is a marketing consultant, mom, and Cub Scout leader.

Index

A

207, 210, 264, 268, 269, 278

Account 13, 14, 37, 38, 104, 156, 187-189, 206, 207, 248

Advertising 128, 151, 227, 260, 261, 281

Apparel 7, 10,-16, 19, 21, 48, 49, 57-59, 62, 63, 80, 95-97, 99, 101-103, 106, 109, 113, 115, 118, 120, 123, 125-127, 141, 147, 148, 151, 190

B

Brand 14, 80, 92, 102, 124, 126, 127, 128, 135, 142, 147, 148, 178, 181, 249, 254, 273

C

Clothing 7-12, 14-16, 20, 21, 56-64, 70, 75, 78, 84, 87, 89, 96, 99, 101, 103, 109, 112, 113, 117-120, 124-128, 130, 131, 133, 137, 140, 142, 143, 162, 163, 169, 175, 193, 196, 210, 224, 250, 251, 256-261

Consumer 10, 105, 107, 112, 114, 123, 172, 182, 282

Creativity 10, 19, 33, 46, 93, 235, 236, 281

Credit 38, 39, 43, 44, 87, 96, 104, 159, 160, 172, 181, 186-188, 204, 206,

E

Embroidery 116, 188, 191, 269

Employee 20, 157, 160, 168, 221, 222, 224, 225, 229-234, 237-241, 269, 270, 275, 277, 279, 281

Event 92, 98, 131, 135, 136, 137, 139, 142, 146-154, 159, 176, 202, 211-223

F

Fashion show 25, 136, 137, 138, 139, 140, 147, 150,-154, 169, 234

Fiber 7, 9, 12, 32, 34, 62, 67, 75-82, 114-117, 162, 198

Fit 8, 15, 41, 55, 59, 88, 89, 118, 131, 136, 163, 186, 196, 197, 214, 215, 220, 234, 240, 258

G

Garment 20, 22, 30, 56, 67, 69, 70-74, 83, 87-89, 91, 93, 103, 106-108, 115-119, 121, 128-130, 132, 151, 167, 175, 185, 186, 194, 196-200, 202, 203, 206, 210-216, 234, 244, 249, 251-254, 257, 258, 262, 282

I

Image 11, 18, 28, 29, 33, 43, 74, 80,
83, 92, 93, 100, 101, 111, 113,
124-128, 130, 131, 136, 137, 147,
152, 170, 177, 182, 202, 212,
237, 244, 258, 261, 262, 273, 281
Income 15, 18, 26, 27, 28, 37, 39, 43,
52, 124, 143, 151, 157, 158, 160,
161, 172-176, 238, 247-249, 255,
268, 269, 272, 274
Insurance 18, 30, 44, 111, 150, 151, 161,
170, 171, 213, 221, 229, 235, 279

L

Label 89, 92, 99-101, 114-119, 125-
127, 137, 142, 196, 197, 202,
220, 237, 249, 275, 278
Leadership 20, 22, 121, 229
License 29, 30, 34, 44, 150, 191, 230
Loans 37, 38, 39, 40, 44, 265, 268, 269
Logo 28, 46, 80, 90, 92, 125-, 128

M

Manufacture 80, 93, 106, 109, 118, 119
Marketing 18, 20- 22, 28, 35, 41-43, 47,
49-51, 54, 74, 83, 95, 97, 98, 113,
123, 125, 127-130, 132-134, 143,
147-151, 155, 159, 166, 169, 170,
175, 176, 186, 189, 194, 207,
234, 243, 245-247, 256, 257, 260-
262, 264, 274
Merchandise 11, 13, 14, 15, 80, 102,
104, 120-122, 125, 150, 151, 160,
161, 202-204, 206, 208-210, 213,
220, 222, 257, 263
Model 25, 57, 70, 83, 88, 130, 131, 137,
138, 139, 141, 156, 170

P

Pattern 12, 20, 64, 70, 74, 78, 79, 84,
88, 89, 91, 92, 93, 116, 154, 163,
166, 192, 197, 222, 258
Policy 30, 44, 84, 110, 150, 159, 203-
209, 232

Price 13, 14, 38, 50, 92, 93, 95-97, 102,
103, 105-108, 120, 132, 156, 163,
173, 175, 176, 180, 185, 192,
196, 198, 209, 216, 250-253, 257,
258, 268, 272-275, 279

Q

Quality 9, 16, 23, 31, 35, 50, 55, 59,
60, 68, 72, 93, 102, 106, 111,
120-122, 125, 127, 163, 193, 200,
203, 212, 214, 218, 220, 235,
236, 239, 243, 247, 248, 254,
259, 262, 264

R

Research 18, 21, 36, 40, 42, 44, 48, 61,
68, 95, 106-109, 124, 129, 151,
158, 163, 180, 250, 252, 254

S

Seamstress 85, 98, 140, 156, 162, 167,
168, 214
Sew 19, 86, 87, 88, 96, 115, 163, 196,
222, 224
Show 12, 15, 23, 25, 46, 64, 67, 72, 74,
83, 96-99, 101-103, 115, 128,
130, 131, 136-141, 147, 150, 151,
153, 154, 169, 173, 174, 182,
192, 194, 234, 235, 236, 264, 277
Skills 19-22, 25, 26, 33, 36, 43, 44, 52,
59, 84, 87, 157, 162, 168, 173,
182, 218, 225, 229, 234, 235,
238, 245, 246
Specialty 14, 16, 56, 57, 64, 115

T

Target market 13, 21, 44, 48, 50, 64, 80,
96, 99-101, 103, 106, 107, 113,
123-127, 129, 131, 132, 136, 144,
147, 159, 170, 175-178, 180-183,
194, 207, 208, 209, 214, 224,
243, 244, 246, 249, 252-254, 258,
260, 261, 273, 281, 282
Textile 90, 109, 117, 162, 191